A Master Guide to
THE ART OF
FLORAL DESIGN

Alisa A. de Jong-Stout A.I.F.D.
with
Hannah Sigur

Photography by Douglas Sandberg
Illustrations by Boris Jeanrenaud

TIMBER PRESS
Portland, Oregon

The botanical illustrations of leaf arrangements, shapes, margins, and venations, which appear in Chapter One, are inspired by Linnaeus's drawings in Philosophia Botanica *(1751).*

Part title page: seed head of *Scabiosa caucasica*.
Frontispiece: David Austin roses.

Published in 2002 by

Timber Press, Inc.
The Haseltine Building
133 S.W. Second Avenue, Suite 450
Portland, Oregon 97204, U.S.A.

Printed in Singapore

Library of Congress Cataloging-in-Publication Data

Jong-Stout, Alisa A. de
    A master guide to the art of floral design / Alisa A. de Jong-Stout with Hannah Sigur; photography by Douglas Sandberg; illustrations by Boris Jeanrenaud.
       p. cm.
    Includes bibliographical references (p.).
    ISBN 0-88192-539-X
    1. Flower arrangement. I. Sigur, Hannah. II. Title

SB449 .J66 2002
745.92—dc21   2001052465

to the Maker of the rose petal

Contents

Acknowledgments, 9
Introduction, 11

Chapter One. Nature's Designs, 15
    The Flower: A Source of Inspiration and Teacher of Design, 15
    Nature's Basic Rules on the Art of Design, 16
    Nature's Principles of Design and Art, 44
    Nature's Designs for Flowers and Leaves, 48

Chapter Two. The Art of Composition, 57
    Concepts: Art and Floral Design, 57
    Contemporary Floral Design: Botanical to Abstract, 64
    Effects of Color and Light, 65
    Considering the Container, 78

Chapter Three. Working with Flowers, 87
    Floral Care, 87
    Construction: Materials and Techniques, 91
    Plants and Bulbs in Floral Design, 97
    Design: Materials and Techniques, 106

Photograph Gallery of Floral Design, 141

Suggested Reading, 223
Index, 225

Acknowledgments

Without all the support over many years from my family, friends, and students, I would never have had the courage for this undertaking, and so the credit for this book belongs to them. My parents, who loved flowers, my Aunt Sabina, who taught me about color, and my ever-encouraging sister-in-law, Emmy, all occupy a special place. The words "thank you" could never suffice for the inspiration of my two American "mothers," Maria Staal and Myrtle Wolf, whose love for flowers is equaled only by their zest for life at nearly ninety. I am forever indebted to Mr. and Mrs. J. Jongstra and family in the Netherlands for their encouragement and all they taught me during the years I trained and worked in their wonderful flower shop, to Ah Sam and Podesta Baldochi, who introduced me to the world of American floral design, and to the horticulture department at Merritt College, where I was privileged to teach for five gratifying years. My partner and dear friend, Philippa Shenon, has given me the gifts of unstinting support and years of joy, as we have worked and shared our love for flowers together. My assistants and students over many years have taught me more than I could teach them. We have grown together.

Filoli Estate National Trust for Historic Preservation, Woodside, California, has been irreplaceable in the realization of this book. Grateful thanks and deep regard go to Lucy Tolmach, director of horticulture; Tom Rogers, curator; and their staff, for their generosity of time, material, place, and advice. Perfect photographic settings were essential to our success. In addition to Filoli, I am indebted to Mrs. Ruth Bancroft and the Bancroft Garden, First Member of the Garden

Conservancy, Walnut Creek; Margaret Lee Blunt; the Crocker Mansion, Hillsborough; DeVera, San Francisco; Alfred and Hedi Schmid-Ernst; Richard and Luisiana Galle; Douglas and Mary Horngrad; and St. Peter's Chapel National Trust for Historic Preservation, Mare Island.

My friends at the San Francisco Flower Mart have been marvelous throughout. Thank you to A. Micheletti & Son, Año Nuevo Nursery, C & M Nursery, Christo Pottery, Daylight Nursery, F. Moggia & Sons, Floral Supply Syndicate, Florist at Large, Gatti Nursery, Gish Endo, Green Valley Growers, J. Podesta & Sons, John Schilling, Junction Wholesale, L. Neve Brothers, Oak Hill Farms, Podesta's of California, Repetto Nursery, Rod McLellan Co., Romano & Son, S. F. Brannan Street Wholesale, Silver Terrace Nursery, Schubert Nursery, Shibata Floral Co., Torchio Nursery, and Western Evergreen. Also in California, I am deeply indebted to Lou Vergeer of B & H Flowers of Carpenteria, Bay City Nursery of Half Moon Bay, California Cut Flower Council, Columbia Pine Cones of Columbia, Davies Dalbok of Living Green, San Francisco, The Gardens at Heather Farms in Walnut Creek, Golden Gate Orchids in South San Francisco, Masse's Pastries of Berkeley, Sun Valley Floral Farms of Arcata, and Willow Mania of Pescadero. Last but not least, profound thanks to Creative Candles of Kansas City, Missouri, and Smithers-Oasis U.S.A., Kent, Ohio.

Special thanks to Margaret Lee Blunt, Milena Boucher, Marilyn Chambers, Cathy Cowman, Susan Fenske, Sam and Marianna Ferris, Paul and Barbara Foster, Robert and Lydia Goshay, Jana Hanavan, Judy Harris, Chong Hatcher, Joyce Haven, Jim and Jacqueline Hermann, Connie Hubbell, Lyena Matene, Janis McNair, Victoria Mournean, Jean Mudge, Eva Poinar-Hecht, Dr. Rudi Schmid, Bärbel Stockhausen, Barbara Thran-Anderson, James Young, and Linda Zin, each of whom in various ways assisted in bringing this book to life and making it a fun and memorable project.

To my patient and loving husband, Loren, and our two wonderful sons, Ted and Peter, who taught me to love life and treasure every moment.

All of these people join me in my wish to let the flower speak, and bring you *A Master Guide to the Art of Floral Design*.

Introduction

No other art is quite like floral design, where medium and subject, interpreter and interpreted are one and the same. Even artist and creation fill unexpected roles: the flowers are the ultimate artists and teachers, and each creative designer merely a pupil. Since the beginning of time, flowers have epitomized beauty and creativity. Their myriad forms, so gentle and fragile, endlessly inspire and challenge. Time spent working with nature's art is always one of enjoyable intimacy. *A Master Guide to the Art of Floral Design* offers an approach that makes the most of such times. This book is for anyone, of any age, and level, in whom flowers inspire a desire to express pure beauty.

Attaining "art" in floral design means thinking with the sensitivity of the world's finest painters of flowers. At times their works were symbolic combinations of blooms never found in the same place or season. Yet, whether inspired by the realm of the imaginary or the real, these painters were first and foremost careful composers. The irrepressible sensuousness in the exquisite blossoms of the paintings by Jan Brueghel or Itō Jakuchū was guided by an urge to highlight the essence of art inherent in the color, form, and grace of nature's jewels. Such awareness resides only in those intimate with real flowers, as indeed these artists are known to have been.

Cutting a flower outdoors to display indoors was conceivably the first and most basic of all artistic impulses. Little else could have been as plentiful, accessible, and easy to use as flowers to beautify daily life. It is just as natural that something so lovely, appearing and disappearing magically with the cycle of the year, would have been regarded by the ancients as the embodiment of divine mysteries. Even in our more sophisticated, less credulous time, none of this has really changed. We bring flowers into every aspect of our lives because they are direct links with the beauty, rhythms, and wonders of nature. They celebrate life itself.

While the passion to create with flowers links us to all who came before us, much has changed. We are luckier than our forebears. With the world appearing smaller and people more traveled and well read than ever, vastly different traditions of floral design that were once unknown are now readily within reach. Modern technology has lengthened the seasons, so that the imaginary bouquets of Old Master paintings can become reality. Hybridizing and the use of greenhouses have eliminated climatic boundaries, placing sun-loving tropicals and shade-loving blooms side by side. Our gardens and floral sources offer more varieties, colors, shapes, and sizes of flowers than ever before. We can explore hue, form, and fragrance unhampered, with pure appreciation.

This cornucopia of opportunities does not come without challenges. To be successful artists, floral designers must know more than their predecessors did. They must concern themselves with the natural behavior of flowers, of course, but also with the more complicated and diverse functions of architectural space, the effects of light and climate, and the choice of floral and other materials. It is wonderful to address this not as a problem but as an invitation to be creative, to make people aware of what the natural beauty of flowers can do to enhance today's life.

Success in any form of design comes from knowledge and respect for materials. The essence of good floral design lies not in any particular style or in bending nature to accommodate the man-made, but in recognizing the flower itself as the ultimate material. On its own, the flower is a superb work of art: look to this gift of nature for guidance. If you are willing to engage it in conversation, the flower will tell you most everything you need to know. If this book can be a source for creative freedom, and pure pleasure, then it will have achieved its goal.

CHAPTER ONE

Nature's Designs

The Flower: A Source of Inspiration and Teacher of Design

In floral design, there is no better teacher than the flower itself. This is the essential maxim. In a flower's perfection, we instinctively recognize the infinite creativity and wisdom of nature. By looking closely at each flower, we take the first step in discovering how best to display its beauty, arrange its placement, and find possible companions in a floral design. Our introduction to this journey of discovery is an exquisite magnolia blossom from the gardens of Filoli in Woodside, California. This blossom exemplifies the basic rules of floral art. The harmony of "color," "form," and "function" that defines this flower is the hallmark of timeless design.

The magnolia is among the most primitive flowers on earth but does not differ in function and basic botanical structure from the more advanced forms. Floral structure remained a tantalizing mystery until an artist's eye and sense of wonderment read the secret: after what must have been years of intimate observation, the German poet Johann Wolfgang von Goethe realized that, whether of a magnolia or an orchid, the petals, sepals, stamens, and pistils that together constitute the flower all evolved from a cluster of modified leaves.

Nature's brilliance as a colorist is shown by the Filoli tree's yellow blossoms, which depart strikingly from those of the typical white or pink magnolia. This difference automatically provokes subtle parallel alterations to all the hues of the plant, from the various parts of the flower itself to the leaves. Thus, in this flower's

The open bloom of *Magnolia* 'Elizabeth',
Filoli Estate, Woodside, California.

soft pristine yellow, deep burgundy-red, and complex of greens, we discover an essential lesson, not only in color harmonies and combinations but also in color composition.

From color we become aware of the array of textures that grace the bloom. The beautiful soft matte of substantial petals, the coarser matte of the stem, the hairy surface of the sepals—all appear clear or muted in hue as the sunlight plays across them. In this we observe too how texture affects color intensity and depth perception, and how a bloom's physical presence attracts the tactile and visual senses.

The magnolia's elegant simplicity of structure underscores how the importance of clarity and the avoidance of the extraneous equal good design. The totality of its parts demonstrates nature's innate sense of rhythm and proportion. In its complete form—buds, flowers, branches—the magnolia contains a wealth of creative inspiration for individual design choices in such areas as height, width, companion plants, containers, and surroundings.

At any level one chooses to work, simple or complex, flowers awaken a creativity and joy that grow boundless with time and practice, ultimately bringing freedom in floral design. This freedom is also a responsibility. For all the achievements of science, we still cannot make or replace a petal. Standing in awe of such fragility and beauty, we in turn cannot help but treat it with respect.

Nature's Basic Rules on the Art of Design

In an art based upon nature, nature is our reality. We cannot duplicate it, nor should we try, but we can benefit limitlessly from its wisdom. As a flower makes the transition from its place in the sun to its position in a work of floral art, it takes on the role of master design teacher.

The flower's secret of success, and therefore the essence of its beauty, lies in its stunning union of color, form, and function. Color and form are used for the purpose of function. The balanced unity of these three factors assures that the flower will survive and reproduce.

We "read" nature using the same descriptive and comprehensive terms that are used to articulate art. Elements are the basic building blocks of art; principles are

Magnolia 'Elizabeth' in bud, Filoli Estate.

the tools we use to assemble these elements. Nature abounds in great examples of the elements and principles of design, as the images in this chapter amply demonstrate. Each can be studied separately. With our instincts thus sharpened, we develop a systematic approach that is genuinely responsive to our medium. Learning to "read a flower" does more than open the door to creative inspiration: it rewards us with answers to questions that arise in planning a concept and directs us with guidelines during construction and evaluation of floral compositions.

COLOR AND LIGHT

Often a floral design begins with choice of color. This at first seems a straight-forward affair: a flower is red or pink or yellow, and foliage is green. In fact, color is variable—and therefore one of the designer's greatest challenges. Colors in nature change constantly in relation to direct surroundings, light, and the tactile qualities of the materials concerned. Observing how color behaves in the environment enriches our sense of color and enhances our sensitivities to the factors that influence it. We therefore begin our analysis of the elements with color and its companion, light.

Color

The plane tree or sycamore (*Platanus* spp.) may seem a strange beginning for a discussion of color, but this tree's softly mottled bark can teach the designer much about color in general and green in particular. Green, like all natural colors, is not always intense or bright. Varied and complex, it comprises many hues, and one plant may display many shades. The greens in the bark of a plane tree are a subtle orchestration in which an overall grayish tone balances the yellowish and bluish greens. Yellow and blue are examples of what Goethe called, respectively, warm and cool colors. These are colors that the human eye seeks in opposition to one another and that we therefore experience as pleasing complementary combinations. The satisfying balance among the different greens illustrates the importance of proportion to the success of any color scheme.

The bark of *Platanus ×hispanica*, the London plane tree, Filoli Estate.

Complementaries or near complementaries appear often in nature, particularly in the color schemes of flowers and plants. Harmony, balance, and blending—nature's preferred methods of organizing color—are inherent within one flower or branch, or between a flower and its surrounding foliage. Together the superb color combinations of the flower and its accoutrements are the natural basis of good floral design. For this reason, the green of foliage can never be ignored but instead must be made to work in concert with the hues of the flowers and its neighboring greens, just as it does in nature. Happily, with its innumerable shades and intensities, green blends and balances with any other natural color. Green is a neutral in floral design, along with white, gray, black, and brown.

Light

With its elegantly curled petals and neutral coloration of green and white, the angel's trumpet datura instructs brilliantly upon the effects of light in nature and therefore in design. In both, the highly complex role that light plays in enticing our perception of shapes and forms cannot be overstated. The datura's sculpted petals show how the direction of light accentuates contours, throwing them into relief by casting shadows. The matte surfaces of the petals absorb light; the shinier surfaces of the leaves reflect it. All this creates effects of depth and texture, even on smooth surfaces. That a floral design may be enjoyed in an artificially lit indoor environment does not alter these basic principles.

The datura also demonstrates the intimate relationship between light and color. The petals tightly folded in the center of the white bloom have a warm, peachy cast; those fully open, in the direct path of the sun, appear bleached. When leaves are partially transparent, they transmit a greenish light upon the surrounding flowers, adding yet another dimension to what we experience as their color. Nothing in nature is one pure hue, and this factor influences the flowers in our designs.

The quality and intensity of light strongly affect our perception of a color as bright, light, or dark. The yellow cast of tropical sunlight makes intense colors dramatic and exciting. In the gray light of the north, the same colors appear harsh. The subdued colors brought to life by northern light appear insipid in southern

Brugmansia arborea, the angel's trumpet datura.

climes. It is as if we view the world through yellow or gray lenses, and with the change of lens, each color assumes a slightly different shade.

The position of the sun, and correspondingly the amount of light experienced, offer lessons in how the elements of our designs should be placed. Colors seem to disappear completely if light shines from behind them, but they become clearly visible when it shines from the front. In the darkness of dawn or dusk, only pale-colored blooms like the datura greet the eye. The rising or setting sun reveals the deeper colors of foliage and landscape. Sunlight at its peak brings out all the colors of the spectrum. With the passage of the seasons, a single landscape displays various blends of possible companion colors to use in our designs, each scheme uniquely beautiful. Nature's every spectrum is a lesson in compatibility.

FORM AND SHAPE

The words "form" and "shape" appear interchangeably in descriptions of flowers and floral design, and indeed their dictionary definitions are nearly identical. While there is nothing inherently incorrect about applying these words randomly, their effectiveness as tools for the description and analysis of the natural world is heightened when they are understood as companion terms in a systematic method of observation. This book will use "form" and "shape" to indicate distinct elements, or building blocks, of nature and floral design. Understanding the two terms as separate concepts enables the designer to plan arrangements with clarity as well as creativity.

Form

When we first encounter this pink magnolia, we do not immediately perceive its blooms, leaves, trunk, and branches as isolated entities. Our eyes take in the whole, comprehending the tree in relation to the world in which it exists, and as we do, our minds and souls are touched. The tree clearly exemplifies form. Form is a kind of totality, incorporating both the tangible and intangible aspects of seeing. After color, form most attracts our attention.

Form in nature contains essential lessons about what underlies the power of expression in a floral design. The magnolia tree could be described simply as a

Magnolia ×soulangeana, Filoli Estate.

mound or a half-round, but a closer look reveals that the strength of its design lies not in this outline but in the growth configuration of its branches. The tree's innate sense of balance, so beautifully displayed in what I call its "dancing skirt," contains an enormous amount of information on how to create space, depth, and freedom in design.

In the photograph the wall and tile roof behind the tree are not only in accord with the tree's color display, they also highlight the magnolia's magnificent form through contrast with their geometry. Looking around, we take in the forms of the nearby conifers and other trees, and last but not least, the contrasting forms and shapes of the blue wisteria, whose great trunk is just visible through the lower branches of the magnolia. The windows of the ballroom, the paths across the lawn, even the sky with its color and light—all are included in our notion of form.

If a dozen people were to observe this tree, each would notice different things and would use the information gained differently. There is no one right, absolute way to comprehend the forms of nature. Emotional sensitivity to form, present in everyone at birth, automatically continues throughout life. We register form psychologically, as protective, threatening, aggressive, tranquil, permanent, or changing. With practice, personal experience of form can be nurtured and refined to feed the imagination and perception and to stimulate creativity. This subtle impossible-to-describe point, where the physicality of the tree meets our emotions, is the seed of what becomes art. It is why, in the final analysis, all we create really is born from nature.

Shape

By learning to read shapes, our eyes come to know the world around us. Everything has a shape. Shapes are the basic building blocks of the structures found in nature, in which universally recognized geometric symbols—triangle, cone, spiral, oval, circle—combine to create the contours of what we see. Children readily engage in this process, but adults often seem to forget it. Yet when we set out to isolate why something in a composition does or does not work, knowledge of shape should be included in our toolchest.

The open blooms of *Magnolia ×soulangeana*, Filoli Estate.

A shape can be measured. It is unchanging, not open to interpretation, and understood by all. Shapes of particular blooms and leaves remain constant in configuration: the shape of the magnolia blossom clearly belongs only to a magnolia, never to a narcissus. A rose silhouette is universally recognized. Soon after beginning to observe flowers, we become sensitive to the various parts of individual blooms, building a reference library of them in our minds.

Shapes give the designer objective information about the flowers in a design. With increasing sensitivity comes the realization that to display its beauty to best advantage, an individualistic bloom like the magnolia needs more surrounding space than a rose. Its shape and coloration make finding suitable companion flowers or even greenery a challenge. Next comes a good reading of its overall growth structure. We observe that the branch supporting the magnolia flower is short and stocky, not long and slender. Analyzing flowers for such practical yet valuable design data may at first seem to detract from the simple joy of appreciating their beauty. As we become more adept in the planning and execution of our designs, however, this process of gathering information becomes instinctive, almost unconscious. Like a concert pianist who has spent hours upon hours learning the notes, by the time of our "performance," the "music" comes not from the notes but from the freedom acquired by having mastered them. This in turn lets the spirit sing.

LINE AND SPACE

Paradoxically, it is space that allows us to read line. Space provides a frame that sparks the life and interest in any design. Vertical, horizontal, diagonal, or curved lines can convey an impression of movement or stasis, stability or instability, weight or lightness, as well as the psychological and emotional qualities associated with these sensations. All lines rely upon the presence of space. Without it, their interaction would be obscured from the eye. Space and line enjoy a symbiotic relationship; one highlights the essential qualities of the other.

Line

This cactus represents a model for the skillful use of line in a design. Its linearity is accentuated by the virtual line created from the shadow of the deep central groove that runs along its length. The specimen is basically vertical, but its slightly diagonal tilt lends a somewhat unsettling effect that creates visual interest and calls

A cactus (*Cereus* sp.) in
fruit, Ruth Bancroft Garden,
Walnut Creek, California.

attention to the plant. The diagonal line is counterbalanced by the roundness and weight of the fruits clinging to the side. Their soft reddish hues balance the green of the cactus, and their volume offsets the flat quality of the plant itself. Spines, radiating like tiny antennae from rows of points, add visual interest and depth to the edges of the plant. All these linear movements and relationships are clearly defined and easily seen with sufficient surrounding space. They demonstrate how a straight line is the most direct and simple of movements, and that any deviation, such as a branch or tilt, will affect the eye and initiate a more active, complex involvement. Line can also detract when not conceived with care; the more complex or crowded the line within a space, the more the eye has to work to see the parts and understand their relationships.

Space

This autumnal branch of rose hips choreographs space. The regularity of the intervals between the hips creates a rhythm that moves the eye, while the hips themselves provide moments of rest, point, and counterpoint, just as in a ballet. This delicate dance is achieved through careful proportion and balance among all the parts, including the surrounding space that allows us to see the whole.

Each rose hip is poised at the tip of a strong yet slender stem. The stems, bare of foliage, highlight the swelling roundness of the hips, just as the hips counterbalance the rhythmic diagonal movement of the stems. The delicately curling remnants of the sepals draw the eye to the tip of each hip and contrast with the simple strength of the stems themselves. The rich red of the hips stands out, not just against the space but also against the bright green of the stems and foliage. Surrounded by a frame of leaves, the entire performance of the hips and stems takes place upon the spare stage of open space, which provides both depth and focus.

PATTERN AND SIZE

In the proportions revealed by pattern and size we discover nature's innate sense of order and come to contemplate our place in it. Size and pattern in the plant world are part of the visible web of nature; our natural attraction for pattern and

A branch of rose hips.

size reflects our own connectedness to that larger order, one that is concrete and consistent. Perhaps that is why designs that ignore nature's patterns are never perceived as beautiful. Pattern and size are the underpinnings of what we understand as beauty: proportions, balance, and rhythm in design. No wonder we find them innately pleasing.

Pattern

Pattern, in essence, is the repetition of what has come before. An entity may replicate a past one, an object may function as a model, an activity may be repeated, or the whole of something may be made up of identical parts. Pattern is often understood within the context of human activity, but the agave shows that it also occurs in the realm of nature. Each new agave is a replication of its parent plant, a stopping point on an endless line of preceding and future generations. The outer form of the agave comes from its inner structure, which relies upon the repetition of one shape, its leaf. These leaves grow from its center outward, each becoming slightly larger as it is pushed by the one emerging from behind. This growth pattern eventually builds a configuration called an equiangular spiral, whose whorls grow ever wider as they proceed. The white edging and geometric lines ornamenting the inner portion of each leaf come from the pressure of the fleshy new leaf folded upon itself before it has unfurled.

The size and shape of each element in the agave relies upon a single extraordinary mathematical relationship of unequal parts called the Golden Ratio, in which a small part stands in relation to a larger part as the larger part does to the sum of them both. Numerically, this creates a proportional progression called the Fibonacci Series (1, 2, 3, 5, 8, 13, and so forth; see the illustration on page 32). The shapes and formal relationships this ratio gives rise to—including the Golden Rectangle, the Golden Section, the Golden Spiral, and the Golden Mean—have been ideals in art and design since ancient times.

Miraculously, the progressive proportions of the Golden Ratio occur consistently throughout nature. It explains how the angles that radiate from the center

Agave victoriae-reginae,
Ruth Bancroft Garden.

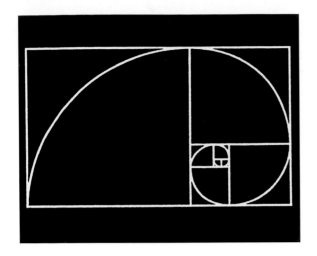

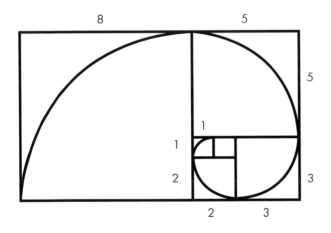

1
1 + 1 = 2
2 + 1 = 3
3 + 2 = 5
5 + 3 = 8
8 + 5 = 13 . . .

The Fibonacci Series.

of the agave's spiral become ever wider by 0.618 as they proceed. It also determines the shape of each leaf and that of the white pattern in its center. Although it is especially easy to see in repetitive configurations such as that of the agave, the Golden Ratio also determines the spirals in a sunflower's center, the curves of a begonia's leaves, and the proportions of an iris's falls.

Nature, in its elegant economical beauty, repeats patterns over and over. While we find the equiangular spiral created by the Golden Ratio in the agave, the pattern in a eucalyptus tree's bark displays the Archimedes (or coil) spiral, in which successive whorls are equidistant from each other. The sphere (or explosion) pattern, which depends on a balance between inward and outward forces, is beautifully evident in a dandelion's seed head and in a lupine's leaves. Trees branch in a logical progression, according to the tree's need to intercept light, radiate heat, shed snow, and withstand wind. The branching patterns of leaves are often so precise as to distinguish one species from another. The geometric pattern known as a fractal can be observed in the bracken fern, whose complex structure is actually the simple repetition of a single irregular form at ever-increasing scale. All these patterns are model frameworks for composition, showing that nature's precision and sense of order underlie all human laws of aesthetics.

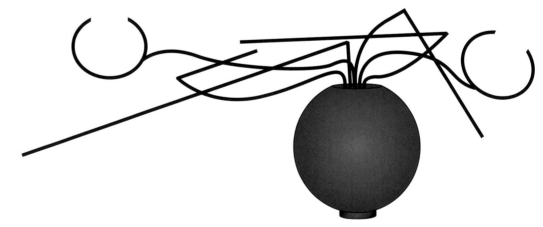

The Golden Ratio in floral design.

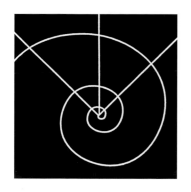

1

2

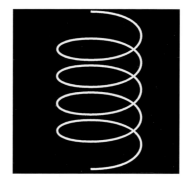

3

4

5

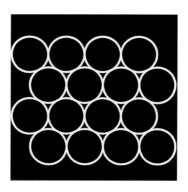

6

1. equiangular spiral
2. Archimedes (or coil) spiral
3. helix (or corkscrew)
4. ripples, flow
5. sphere (or explosion)
6. packing, stacking
7. branching
8. fractals

7

8

Nature's patterns.

Size

Size is not simply a matter of length, height, or width. It is also comprehended through volume, weight, density, and color. Even this photograph cannot obscure the grandeur of the agave, among the largest creations of the plant world. We can see its volume in the fleshy thickness of its leaves. Their draping heaviness conveys sheer weight. Pale gray-green coloration and flat surface texture increase the impression of largeness by reflecting light, their effects accentuated by the simple geometry of the triangulations that divide the planes of each leaf. The spines along their edges articulate like a natural measuring stick. Proceeding from the base toward the tip, spaced progressively farther apart according to the numerical ratio of the Fibonacci Series, their calibration exaggerates each leaf's already impressive length.

SEASON AND CLIMATE

Whatever its origin, a flower remains for us the ideal symbol for life's progress, communicating each season's special message—new life in spring, full bloom in summer, abundance in fall, hope and rest in winter. Certain bulbs and soft new green leaves never fail to bring spring to mind. Berries, seedpods, and chrysanthemums, red, orange, and yellow leaves—all seem right only in autumn. We and the flower remain linked to time. Today, season and geography no longer constrain designers in their selection of plant material. But before flowers from different climates, seasons, and hemispheres are combined, it is necessary to know their life cycles, individual characteristics, and the way each behaves in a floral design.

Season

Three images of a scabiosa bloom exquisitely portray three seasons in the short life of a flower: bud, bloom, and seedpod. At each stage, its captivating beauty is complete and distinctive in itself. The scabiosa bud, carried on a long arching stem, is a symphony of expectant greens, from deep bluish and soft yellow to pale mint and nearly white; a ring of slender hairy sepals and tightly folded immature petals frame a half-globe of tiny buds, reminiscent of a kitten's furry paws. In the

Agave franzosinii, Ruth Bancroft Garden.

Scabiosa caucasica, the
pincushion flower, in bud,
bloom, and seed head.

open bloom, the petals explode into a ruffled tutu of blue-lavender fading to nearly white, set off by delicate pink anthers; the minute hairs of the tiny green buds make a geometric netting of little stars. On the seedpod, poised on a now-straightened stem, the buds have unfurled to form the tiny geodesic globe of a seed head. With its star-shaped pistils of burgundy nestled in pleated, papery florets of bright yellow-green and translucent white, striped in deep red, the mature scabiosa epitomizes the concept of complementaries.

The flower's journey from bud to seed is a miracle of immortality. This defining quality of transformation makes floral design a uniquely lively art, for we have the possibility of a complete metamorphosis within the vase life of an arrangement. Within the lifetime of a design, poppy buds mature to bloom and pod, tulip stems curve with age, rose petals change color and fall. Each stage has its own captivating beauty, complete and distinctive. Understanding nature's underlying cycles is central to successful floral design. Each flower within an arrangement will retain an independent life cycle that may or may not coordinate with those of its companions. While this makes selecting combinations all the more challenging, utilizing this characteristic not only can prolong the life of the design, it respects the very essence of the flower.

Climate

Like most tropical blooms, the ornamental ginger is a floral powerhouse. It takes a special kind of strength to thrive in equatorial climes, where extremes would overwhelm something more delicate. The bold contours of its strong leathery leaves and the compactly architectural composition of its fleshy petals can withstand relentlessly hot sun and crushingly heavy rains. Where a subtly colored northern flower would appear washed out and inconspicuous in the intense yellow of tropical sunlight, the ginger's brilliant red is vibrantly appealing. Such conspicuousness assures it will be noticed, increasing its chances for successful pollination.

The ornamental ginger and scabiosa beautifully demonstrate why the relationship of climate and season is always a factor in designs. A flower will retain its character no matter what circumstance it finds itself in. The scabiosa has a gentle character; it is lovely at any stage of its life cycle and will therefore combine easily

Ornamental ginger (*Zingiber* spp.).

with other blooms. But the ginger can be used only at its peak; the physical qualities assuring its survival result in a presence of such power and distinction that, like
other "noisy" flowers, it does not mingle easily and works best in bold designs that
allow it ample space. A floral design may combine many blooms whose natural
environments have fostered widely disparate physical traits. Noting and composing
according to these differing natural qualities give expressive vitality to our work.

TEXTURE AND FRAGRANCE

For all their fragility, flowers spare no effort in their quest to entice. Colors from
pale to lush catch the eye. The fresh damp scent of mingling foliage and bloom
graces forest and garden air and positively jolts us in the confines of a florist shop.
Branches knock together when tossed by the wind. A petal may excite the tongue
with its peppery taste. For me, nothing could have shown the irresistible sensuality
of flowers better than the sight of my son the day I found him, at age two or three,
in the garden with a little friend. Hand in hand, they romped from flower to
flower, kissing the blooms. "You might hurt them, blow kisses instead," I
cautioned, and so they blew their kisses to the flowers. Seeing, smelling, hearing,
tasting, and touching are all part of the job that insects and birds perform for
flowers every day. We are lucky. We do it for pleasure.

Texture

The festive pincushion protea is an ideal teacher of texture. Its ribbonlike petals
of red and white candy-stripe have a leathery stiffness combined with a surface
quality reminiscent of natural silk. The white hairs exuberantly fringing them are
lustrous from the sides, fuzzy at the tips. Stiff, glossy stamens shoot through the
curling petals like bursts of yellow fireworks. Not to be outdone, leaves cup the
exploding bloom in a crisp aureole of shiny dark green. Dull and glossy, coarse
and fine, hairy and smooth, soft and tough—all the basic surface qualities we
encounter in flowers are articulated with superb clarity by the protea, whose
brilliant coloration exemplifies the effects of texture on color. Color on a shiny
surface does not have the same intensity and depth as the identical hue on a matte
surface. A very close look at the surface of the protea's petals reveals minute bumps;

The pincushion protea (*Leucospermum* spp.).

these tiny textural subtleties create color gradation through infinitesimal variations of light and shadow. Whether refined or bold, interesting textural combinations are found in all flowers. These same textures can suggest which blooms and foliage to combine in a design and how to integrate the design with its container and surroundings.

Fragrance

Scent identifies the exquisite lily of the valley as much as its tiny spikes of opalescent white bells and narrow leaves of deepest glossy green. A whiff of its perfume, and its image automatically rises before the eye. So it is with a rose or a jasmine. Scent is not always present in a bloom but utterly evocative when it is. It can be delicate and inviting, refreshing and invigorating, or downright brazen and overbearing. Its effects are intangible, emotional, and individual as well as physical. Scent can spark the recollection of a place, person, or experience with which it is associated in the mind of the one who encounters it. Perhaps even more than form, scent can spur memory, inspire creativity, and excite the emotions. It can bring joy, melancholy—or even a headache. Scent, the most elusive element in our encounter with flowers, can be most powerful.

With its profound role in our experience of a flower, scent cannot be ignored in a floral design. It is not an incidental accent, but integral to companion blooms, the space in which a design is to be used, and the purpose for which it is intended. To combine a lily of the valley with another strongly scented bloom can induce an argument between the two, overwhelm the senses, and detract from the rest of the composition. In a confined space, strongly scented flowers can be intensely egotistical. But in the right circumstances, when their fragrance is given room to spread, they add a unique pleasure to our encounter that nothing else can match.

Convallaria majalis, the lily of the valley.

Nature's Principles of Design and Art

Rules and theories are good for the beginning hours; during the mature hours, problems are easily solved due to the knowledge built up from the beginning hours.

JOHANNES ITTEN

The elements of design are only the beginning of what we learn by reading flowers and plants. Reading also reveals that when nature creates according to its essential triad of color, form, and function, it does so in ways that accord with established principles employed in structure and composition. The American Institute of Floral Designers (A.I.F.D.) uses these principles to assess floral design, dividing them into primary and secondary levels. In the learning environment of the classroom, it is easier to combine under one heading those principles whose roles are related, in the execution and evaluation of a design.

UNITY

The principle of unity is nature's true gift to design. A brilliant union of color, form, and function, the flower subordinates every other principle to this goal. Unity is the secret of its survival and the source of its attraction.

Not only does every component of a flower have a distinct purpose, but also the different hues, shapes, textures, and aromas that constitute the bloom must work together, to meet the demands of the flower's environment, or else the flower fails to reproduce. The fragrance and color of a bloom work with the shape of petals so that an insect or bird, once attracted, can do its job. Nature's concept of integrated relationship can also be applied to floral design: the link among flowers, container, and surroundings is the basis by which we meet the function, or purpose, of a composition. A unified composition is a successful and beautiful one.

Unity may be one of harmony or one of diversity. Unity of harmony possesses a satisfying sense of oneness as its aesthetic quality. Unity of diversity produces a sense of wholeness through a complex interplay of agreement or adaptation among unlike things.

BALANCE, PROPORTION, SCALE, AND DEPTH

Balance is a state of equilibrium or stability. In a flower, proper balance among parts ensures the flower will succeed. A rose with too many petals for its surrounding conditions will fail to open and will never be fertilized. In design, balance is constructed using interior rhythms and variety among the elements of a design, such as color, texture, and size. If all elements have equal visual force, the composition will appear static and dead. Balance may be symmetrical, in which both sides of the design appear equal in weight or size, or asymmetrical, in which one side appears to dominate. Asymmetrical balance relies upon a pivot point for visual stability.

Proportion and scale are comparative relationships of size, quantity, and degree of emphasis. They exist among the materials within a composition, between the composition and its container, and between both together in relation to the surrounding environment, with the goal that these interrelationships be experienced as aesthetically and psychologically pleasing.

Depth includes dimensionality and perspective. All flowers and plants possess a degree of depth; no design will ever be completely two-dimensional. The degree of depth, however, may be either real or perceived. Actual depth is achieved by the placement of materials at different points in an arrangement, from front to back. Illusional depth is created using directional light or through the juxtaposition of colors, textures, and shapes, some that visually recede, others that come forward.

CONTRAST, OPPOSITION, AND TENSION

Contrast, opposition, and tension refer to emphases achieved by juxtaposing strikingly different lines, forms, textures, sizes, shapes, or colors. These forces enhance a composition by creating dynamism of expression and movement, luring the observer into dialogue with the floral design. Counterbalancing these principles requires careful editing and arrangement of materials, with special attention to proper spacing; crowding diminishes their effect.

DOMINANCE, EMPHASIS, ACCENT, AND FOCAL POINT

Dominance is a visual principle of organization in which one aspect of a design, such as color, shape, texture, line, or size, draws special attention or has prominence. This emphasis causes the eye to rest momentarily as it moves around the design, a pause that is essential for prolonging the viewer's engagement and interest. Care must be taken not to throw the composition out of balance by too strong a dominance or emphasis.

Accent is a detail of dominance or emphasis, one that is proportionately small in relation to the whole design. By providing a point of attraction, it enhances the entirety.

Focal point (or focal area) is one that is proportionately large in relation to the whole design, creating one or more centers of attention in the composition.

RHYTHM, TRANSITION, REPETITION, AND VARIATION

Rhythm, a visual sense of natural movement, is usually achieved by repetition, gradation, or proportional sharing of diverse parts. It encourages the eye to travel around and through the components of a design. Rhythm gives liveliness and grace; it is essential to our medium, because indoor design lacks the effects of wind and sunlight by which nature creates movement.

Transition is a passage from one area to another through changes in line, form, color, texture, space, pattern, or size.

Repetition is the use of like elements within a composition. It re-creates the sense of order found throughout nature, which we therefore experience as pleasing. Without it, the eye will be confused and overwhelmed with detail.

Variation is the use of minor differences within a harmony, rhythm, or group of materials that are generally similar. Variation prevents monotony.

A close reading of any flower reveals that it harmonizes several or all of these rules. Yet, sublimely gifted artist that it is, every flower delightfully demonstrates that rules are made to be broken. In each of the nearly one million floral species and cultivars known to grace our planet, not even two blossoms are identical. Like human beings, each flower possesses a life and an identity, a flicker of personality to be discovered.

This fact, daunting at first, can also spark a sense of adventure, for in such extraordinary variety lies the key to a deeper understanding of our medium and the creative freedom that such awareness brings. It tells us that being a stickler is a sure path to an unimaginative, formulaic result, but that if we approach floral design the way nature does the flower, rules become guides by which we develop intuition for what is "right." If, like nature, we never forget the integrity of the blooms we use, our designs will show their art, whether our work is botanical or abstract.

Let us turn once again to the magnolia at Filoli, this time as a teacher bent on kindly reviewing for us the principles of design, first by definition and then as they relate to the tree itself and to the composition of the photograph as a whole.

The magnolia as a teacher of the principles of design, Filoli Estate.

Unity relates to the overall form of a design or the sum of its parts. When we perceive the principle of unity, we feel complete. By its very being, this pink magnolia, in full, magnificent array, is the perfect "floral design" for welcoming guests to the Filoli ballroom behind it. A composition is unified when it works together with all the elements in the space around it, as this magnolia does to great effect.

Balance, proportion, scale, and depth relate to the planning and execution of a design. A plant cannot survive without balance, proportion, and scale in relation to its function and environment. So it is with floral design. The flower-laden branches of the magnolia, complete with their "dancing skirt," rely upon an elegant balance that is proportional to the scale of the tree. The flower buds invite the observer to look inside the tree and discover the placement and design of its branches. The relationship of the tree to the wisteria and the architectural elements is spatial as well as formal; we take in both the tree's beauty and its surroundings. All actively engage us, setting the tone for any festivities that may be taking place inside.

Contrast, opposition, and tension relate to visual stimulation. The principles of contrast, opposition, and tension abound in nature. An encounter with them sparks our attention. The magnolia beckons with contrasts of color, texture, and shape, within the blooms, between the blooms and the buds, and against the trunk and branches. Opposition occurs between the tree's soft rounded contours and the hard flat geometry of the building and path, to say nothing of seeing the pinks of the tree against the blue of the sky. Such tensions make us aware of the distinctiveness of each element.

Dominance, emphasis, accent, and focal point relate to visual respite. Involving the elements of color, shape, texture, line, and size, these principles are among nature's most useful means of catching and holding the eye, thereby providing an essential visual resting place. While the focal point lies in the center of the magnolia tree, its flowers in full bloom dominate; those still in bud create welcome accents. The tree in turn dominates the setting: its spring floral display and sheer scale are the focal point of the entire composition. The wisteria's color and shape are accents that invite the viewer to take in the rest of the surroundings.

Rhythm, transition, repetition, and variation relate to movement. These important principles exist in the passage of the seasons, in the movement of wind and water, in the weather, in the life cycle of the flower, and in the colors, shapes, and forms of all things. The dancing branches of the magnolia are a natural example of the principle of rhythm in design. The repetition and variation of shape and color in the flowers and branches encourage the eye to move from one to the next, in seamless transition. The variations of form between the magnolia's rounded contours, the nearby climbing wisteria vine, and the shape of the windows provide unifying repetitions supported by color transitions: the tree blossoms harmonize with the reddish brown of the brick and the pale blues of the wisteria vine. All work together to encourage the eye to move around the composition.

Nature's Designs for Flowers and Leaves

The floral designer need be concerned with only a few basic plant characteristics. All flowering plants are angiosperms, characterized by their protected, enclosed seeds. Angiosperms have two subclasses: a flower is either a monocotyledon (monocot) or a dicotyledon (dicot). Monocots have only one leaf when the seed first sprouts; dicots sprout with two. In a monocot, petals and sepals look alike, leaves are in one piece and of a simple shape with parallel veins, and the plant is low-growing, with few branches; orchids, lilies, and grasses are typical monocots. A dicot has distinct petals and sepals, leaves in various shapes with networks of veins, and branching stems; like most trees, our magnolia is a dicot, as are roses, violets, and chrysanthemums. Being able to recognize a flower as a monocot or dicot is a wonderful tool for discovering the differences between simple and complex, restful and animated designs.

All flowers conform to the same basic structure because they share the same function: they exist to reproduce the plants they adorn. In the very center of each flower are one or more female reproductive organs, or pistils, each consisting of a stigma, style, and ovary. These are surrounded by the male organs, or stamens, in which a slender filament bears an anther. Together these organs are the reproductive heart of a blossom. They are nestled in the perianth, which is a union of two parts: a base, or calyx, composed of petal-like structures called sepals, and a corolla of petals, which emerges from the base.

Most flowers are supported by a stem. The relationship between the stem and the number of flowers it bears is called the inflorescence, of which several configurations are possible.

A leaf manufactures nutrients for the plant. It may originate from a growing point either on the tip or sides of a stem or at the base of a flower, but many further variations of these two types of leaf may occur. In the basic leaf, the main part, or blade, joins the plant by means of the petiole. The veins of a leaf blade are usually arranged in one of three ways: veins may be parallel, veins may radiate from a base, or they may be arranged with a central midrib and branching secondary and tertiary veins. A blade may even lack visible veins altogether.

Leaves occur in two basic configurations, simple and compound. Simple leaves are undivided and have one blade and one petiole. Compound leaves are subdivided into leaflets, united either on a common stem or a shared base.

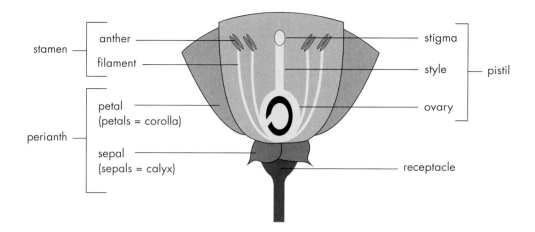

Structure of the flower.

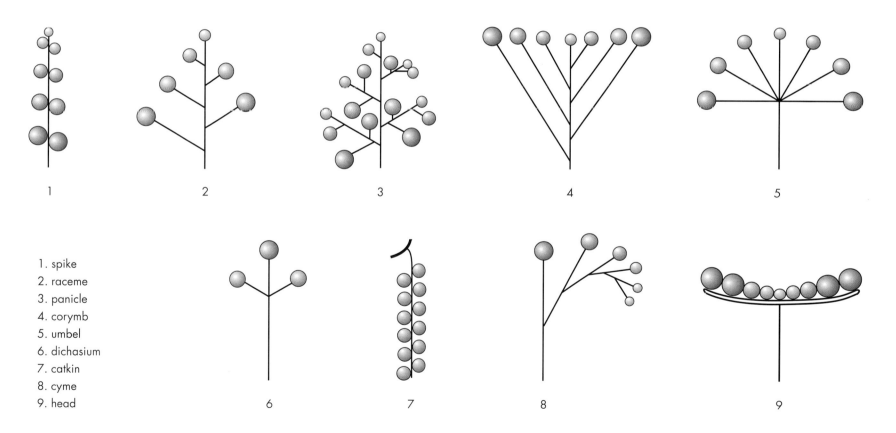

1. spike
2. raceme
3. panicle
4. corymb
5. umbel
6. dichasium
7. catkin
8. cyme
9. head

Types of inflorescences.

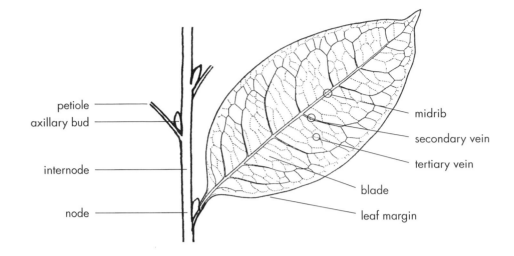

petiole

axillary bud

internode

node

midrib

secondary vein

tertiary vein

blade

leaf margin

Structure of a leaf with central midrib and branching veins.

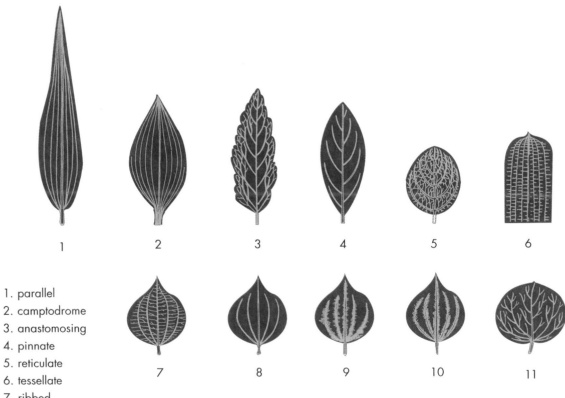

1

2

3

4

5

6

1. parallel
2. camptodrome
3. anastomosing
4. pinnate
5. reticulate
6. tessellate
7. ribbed
8. conspicuous
9. prominent
10. furrowed
11. laciniate

7

8

9

10

11

Leaf venations.

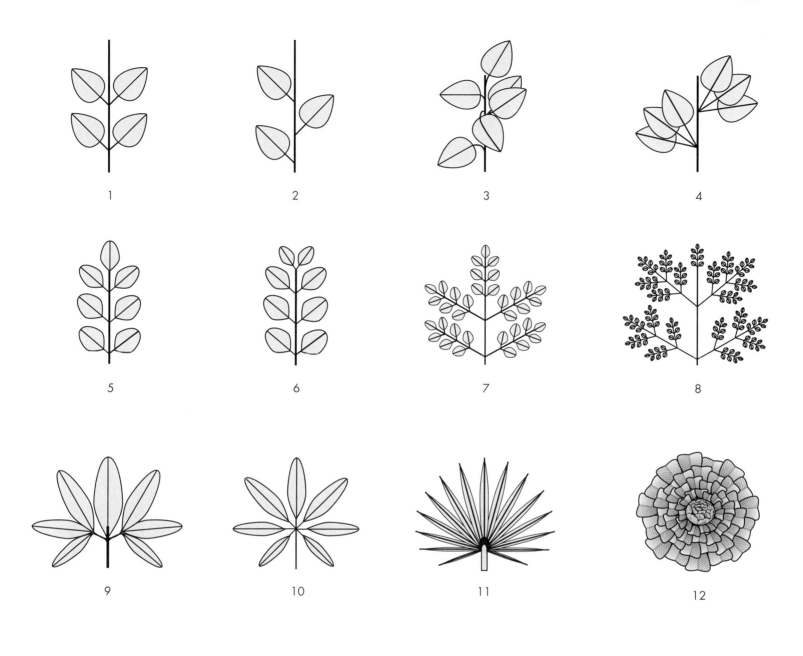

1. opposite
2. alternate
3. scattered
4. clustered
5. imparipinnate
6. paripinnate
7. bipinnate
8. tripinnate
9. pedate
10. digitate
11. palmate
12. rosulate

Simple and compound leaf arrangements.

Leaves take countless shapes, resembling, among other things, swords, ribbons, eggs, fans, hearts, and palms. Their margins may be smooth, notched, fringed, or lobed. Their surfaces may be hairy or hairless. Leaves appear in innumerable shades of green, as well as white, red, and other hues, and in combinations. Leaf shapes, patterns, textures, and colors are part of the botanical identity of flowers and are therefore of great importance to a design.

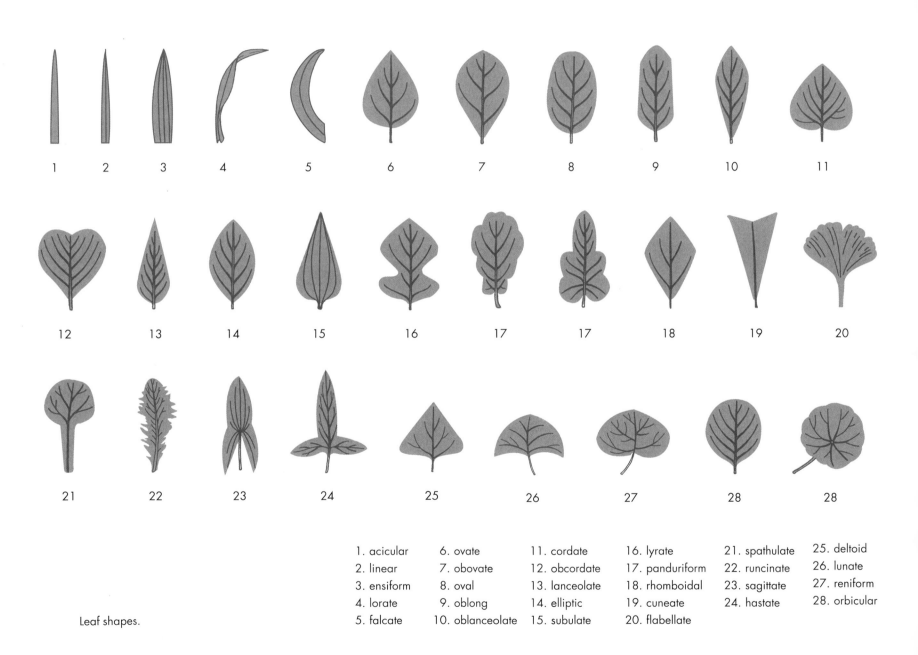

Leaf shapes.

1. acicular	6. ovate	11. cordate	16. lyrate	21. spathulate	25. deltoid
2. linear	7. obovate	12. obcordate	17. panduriform	22. runcinate	26. lunate
3. ensiform	8. oval	13. lanceolate	18. rhomboidal	23. sagittate	27. reniform
4. lorate	9. oblong	14. elliptic	19. cuneate	24. hastate	28. orbicular
5. falcate	10. oblanceolate	15. subulate	20. flabellate		

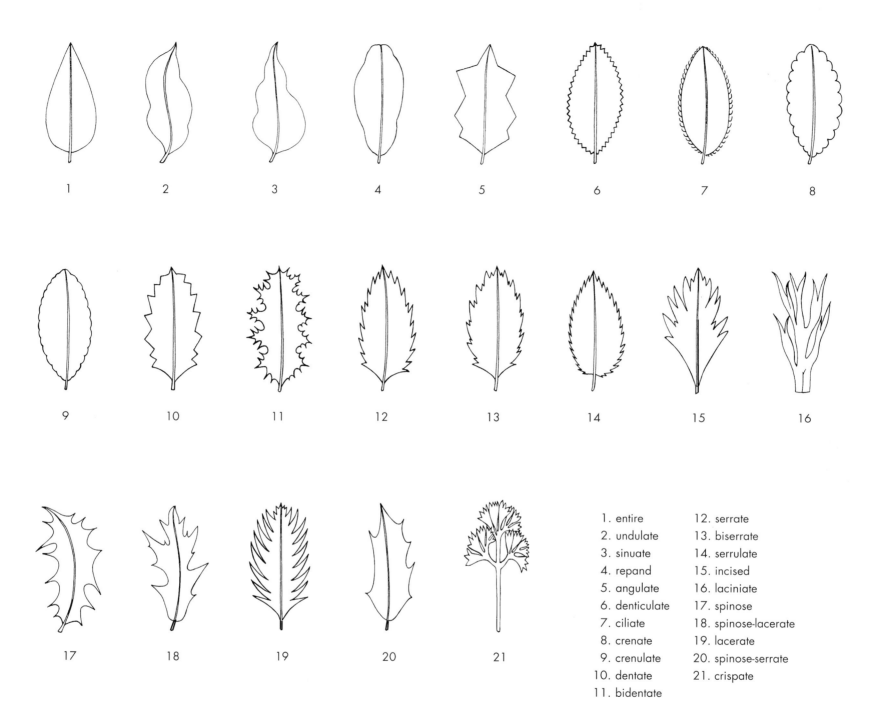

1. entire
2. undulate
3. sinuate
4. repand
5. angulate
6. denticulate
7. ciliate
8. crenate
9. crenulate
10. dentate
11. bidentate
12. serrate
13. biserrate
14. serrulate
15. incised
16. laciniate
17. spinose
18. spinose-lacerate
19. lacerate
20. spinose-serrate
21. crispate

Leaf margins.

1. puberulous
2. villous
3. velutinous
4. floccose
5. papillose
6. verrucose
7. peltate hairs
8. squamose
9. lepidote

Leaf surfaces.

1   2   3

4   5   6

7   8   9

This book will sometimes refer to a plant by its scientific name, according to the Linnaean binomial system, as well as by its common name. The binomial system consists of two words: the first refers to the genus (a group of closely related plants) to which the plant belongs; the second, or specific epithet, identifies the species within the genus. The genus and the specific epithet together make up the species name. Often a plant will be a hybrid involving one or more species of its genus or a slight variation of a single species; these cultivar ("cultivated variety") names are given in single quotation marks. For the floral designer, both the scientific and common names of a plant are useful for more than simple identification and communication. They are an essential means of organizing in our minds the information that we observe.

When one becomes familiar with the flower in its natural role, one sees it differently. Once basic information about structure, physical characteristics, life cycle, and natural environment is internalized, this new knowledge instinctively becomes a reference and consideration. The conscious eye and mind are freed to explore subtleties of color, texture, shape, and structure that would otherwise have been overlooked.

By reading our medium—the flower—and using it as paint, brush, and canvas, we find the unity of color, form, and function, the stunning triad that underlies every successful floral composition. The more a designer truly sees and knows about a flower, the more creativity is enhanced. This, together with a blossom's limited lifespan, makes the art of floral design a challenge yet tremendously rewarding, for in its lessons lies the secret of life, joy, and beauty.

CHAPTER TWO

The Art of Composition

Concepts: Art and Floral Design

Flowers have fascinated us forever. Their beauty always makes them the perfect symbol for the joyous occasions and milestones of life. In earlier ages, they were woven inseparably into the fabric of society. Flowering plants provided food and medicine necessary for survival; science and technology relied upon them; and as objects of trade, they brought prosperity and widened horizons by helping to link distant cultures. Literature, art, and archaeology show that over the centuries, something akin to "designing with flowers" has been practiced in many different places and taken numerous forms. It is wonderful to know just how widespread and ancient an art it is. Much has been lost to the unrecorded past, but we can look to three great recorded traditions of floral design from China, Japan, and Europe. Each treated the flower with honor and took seriously the practice of working with it. Contemporary floral design owes them a great debt.

The Chinese, Japanese, and European traditions contrasted with one another in significant ways, but they all concerned themselves with three key concepts—"color," "form," and "appreciation." In each style, one factor would dominate while the other two played supporting roles in descending order of importance, according to the special needs of the society to which that tradition belonged. Consequently, each had different determinants of what made a "successful design." A brief look through their eyes will show us some wonderful ways to read a bloom and poise us to look beyond them to the inspiration that they ultimately share.

Little Bouquet in a Clay Jar by Jan Brueghel.
Courtesy Kunsthistorisches Museum, Vienna.

CHINESE AND JAPANESE FLORAL DESIGN

Historically, Chinese floral design placed "appreciation" above form and made color the last concern. The idea of appreciation corresponds to our concept of function because it required that a design serve a special social purpose. The importance of the relationship between floral arts and people was even apparent in certain technical terms, which had been borrowed from societal roles and applied to composing with blooms.

Conceived around a language of flowers, a traditional Chinese arrangement communicated a message about a particular person or the larger society to those who viewed it. Individual blooms and foliage, and their combinations, were symbolic expressions of nature's inner harmony. Through appreciation of flowers, the same harmony could be encouraged in people, who were, after all, part of nature themselves. A successful composition conveyed the designer's most profound thoughts with subtlety. Floral design itself was valued as one of the four skills of a refined life, the hallmark of a cultured person.

The term "ikebana," the best-known word for traditional Japanese floral design, has many shades of meaning. It refers not just to arranging flowers but also to the concept of "giving them life," and suggests that a special spirit of intimacy with flowers may be achieved through veneration of their perfect beauty. In highlighting this beauty, the traditional practitioner of ikebana emphasized "form," so much so that the designer sometimes trimmed foliage or blooms, artificially refining contours with the aim of assembling an idealized whole. After form followed appreciation of meaning, corresponding to our concept of function, and lastly, color. This sensitivity to form gave birth to many different schools of floral design.

The importance of form may be linked to the special relationship floral design bore to its traditional architecture and painting. The focal point of a Japanese room was a special alcove called the "tokonoma," intended solely for the display of a carefully selected painting and an equally carefully conceived composition of blooms. As a deliberate pairing, each had to complement the other in particular ways and be appropriate to the season, occasion, or celebration. Yet, the paintings were often rendered in black ink, the sparsely furnished room itself had little color, and above all, the interior light was filtered and subdued. Surrounding shadows reduced the visibility of floral color and the details of the painting. Only form retained immediate impact. In emphasizing the relationship between an arrangement and its surroundings, both physical and emotional, ikebana presents a classic example of design dominated by form.

EUROPEAN FLORAL DESIGN

Unlike the concepts extensively developed and recorded by the Chinese and Japanese, the less homogenous culture of Europe offers only scattered literary references and no uniform theory concerning floral design. Yet, we have only to scan the rich expanse of visual arts to discern a strikingly consistent way of thinking about it. Beautiful mosaics and frescoes depicting baskets of fruits and blooms survive from Roman times, but perhaps it is more appropriate to seek the origins of this tradition in the culture that emerged after the turmoil of the Dark Ages. Countless images on illuminated manuscripts, engravings, textiles, paintings, and porcelains show that from the Middle Ages onward, floral design progressed with ever greater vitality through the Renaissance, Enlightenment, and Victorian periods. All evidence points to a profound fascination with the immediate impact of "color," expressed through the massing of blooms.

Color has great meaning in Western civilization. From earliest times, it has dominated the pictorial arts. Architecture, emphasizing the introduction of light by means of large windows and pale walls, naturally highlighted the colors of things indoors. European taste inclined toward color to brighten and beautify interiors. The stained-glass windows of European cathedrals and monasteries reveal at a glance the association of color and light with the divine.

Following closely on the heels of color came the notion of appreciation, and lastly, form. To substantiate these rankings, we turn both to literary evidence and to the visual clues offered by the significance of floral still lifes in our artistic tradition. Floral symbolism played an important role in many eras and lives on in the association of certain blooms and plants with specific occasions and times of year. Fragrant bouquets were placed in homes and worn to ward off disease. Cultivated flowers, introduced through trade with foreign lands and acquired at enormous expense, signified the wealth and status of their owners. When people did pay attention to formal aspects of arranging, they tended to avoid artifice and instead delighted in abundance and profusion by displaying flowers according to their natural growth habits.

SEEING THROUGH THE EYES OF ARTISTS: Jan Brueghel and Itō Jakuchū

Floral design is an art like painting or sculpture. It combines some of the qualities of both, and shares with them the compositional challenges of color, form, and shape. Artists in all three disciplines have in common an acutely sensitive eye for the surrounding world, in which they find continuous inspiration. It is no surprise then that some of the most adept pupils of the flower were artists who specialized in painting them. By taking a moment to ponder the very different work of two gifted artists, Flemish painter Jan Brueghel (1568–1625) and Itō Jakuchū (1716–1800) of Japan, we can gain insight into what it means to observe and how to make use of what we learn. "Reading a flower" is not such a new idea after all.

One of a highly cultured family of painters stretching at least two generations before him and two after, the extraordinarily talented Jan Brueghel richly deserves the sobriquet "The Flower Brueghel." His still lifes owe their intense vitality to consummate color and miniaturist techniques that began with his childhood mastery of watercolor. As a young apprentice, he learned to make pigments and paints, many of which relied upon flowers for their color. The adult Brueghel enjoyed the privilege of painting in the extensive gardens of the Archduke of Antwerp, who collected rare flowers. The religion of his day imbued flowers with symbolism. In short, they permeated every aspect of Brueghel's life—technical, intellectual, and spiritual. His vivid depictions of them gave concrete form to the cosmopolitanism of the Renaissance.

The blooms generously massed in Brueghel's *Little Bouquet in a Clay Jar* (see page 56) epitomize not just European still life painting but European floral design as well. What at first seems a random selection of flowers is revealed under close examination to be the product of careful planning and minute attention to detail.

A classic example of the European emphasis on color over appreciation and form, the bouquet's predominant scheme of blue and yellow beautifully demonstrates a compositional framework based on color contrasts. Indeed, we have only to look at the opulently ruffled blue iris to see that nature suggested this combination. Brueghel adds a scattering of red and orange flowers for visual spark, blending them into the whole by including blooms in related tints of peach and soft pink. The delicate pastels and neutral whites, in particular the narcissus with their yellow centers, provide color transitions without competing for attention. Reading nature's lessons in the iris may well have led Brueghel to this brilliantly simple method for uniting the miscellany of unrelated floral shapes, sizes, and textures found among the blooms, container, and surroundings.

The flowers themselves, at the peak of perfection, appear in a fascinating combination of realism and artifice. Brueghel portrays them with botanical precision as well as deep insight into their individual habits of growth, placing each to be easily visible. Gracefully tumbling according to each stem's natural curvature, the blossoms pose at various angles. The large ones stand out with immediate effect, set off to advantage against a wealth of small ones that require more careful perusal to be fully comprehended. Drawn into the composition, we see the sepals on the undersides of some flowers, the interior stamens of others, petals that are translucent and soft, stiff and waxy, feathery or curled. Different types of inflorescences are rendered with care. In this subtle fashion, Brueghel captures and holds our sense of wonder.

Brueghel usually painted directly from nature, without preparatory drawings or oil sketches. His devotion was such that he would wait for a rare flower to bloom. The softly contoured form of the arrangement arises from his intimate knowledge of the physicality and behavior of each blossom. Yet what we see is not a garden-gathered bouquet. Narcissus, which have much shorter stems than irises and roses, appear unnaturally high in this composition. The muscari, fritillarias, tulips, narcissus, and hyacinths are flowers of early spring. Bearded irises and roses open later in the season, while lilies, carnations, and marigolds appear in summer and early autumn. Some are humble field flowers, and others expensive cultivated blooms. The cast of light throws the blossoms into deep relief, making them glow against the neutral hues of the dark foliage, container, and tabletop. This juxtaposition of beloved flowers from all seasons and classes possesses an air of magic: in Brueghel's day, irises and roses had religious significance, and Paradise was understood as the place where all the flowers of the year bloomed simultaneously. While we cannot know with certainty the artist's intent and thus the painting's original function, the joy that emanates from this lovely assemblage transcends time.

A long line of wholesale greengrocers with little education or sophistication improbably produced one of Japan's most brilliant painters, the reclusive and spiritual Itō Jakuchū. He seems not to have begun painting until adulthood, when able to leave the family business. Uninterested in success, wealth, or luxury, Jakuchū took refuge in religion and became a lay monk. He lived alone, a celibate bachelor absorbed in perfecting his art. The exquisite paintings that have dazzled everyone since were devotional works.

As a Zen Buddhist, Jakuchū found his deepest inspiration in the glories of familiar natural phenomena. The name of his studio, "Shin'enkan," referred to the beauty of the surrounding green vistas, the sight of which released his spirits from earthly cares. He lovingly depicted ordinary animals and plants coexisting in harmony, their peacefulness conveying his belief in the essential unity of all living things. Jakuchū saw every flower, bird, grass, and insect as the possessor of a unique innate spirit, which he believed could only be discovered through constant, close observation.

Rooster, Hen and Hydrangeas was the fruit of Jakuchū's exceptional technique, gentle spirit, and intimate accord with living things. Painting in mineral colors on silk allowed no modifications, but Jakuchū proceeded with such confidence and control that the pale lines delineating the flowers consist merely of bare fabric. Constructing each hydrangea bract by bract, grass cluster blade by blade, bird feather by feather, he brilliantly replicates the relationship between shape and form in nature. He contrasts the notched edges, geometrically aligned veins, and leathery consistency of the hydrangea leaves with the crisp simplicity of the peony's foliage and the softness of the grasses. His sophisticated color scheme relies upon the subtle kinship between shades of blue and green blended with neutral white, brown, and black; red draws the eye to the birds.

Superb composition sustains the impact of this wealth of detail. Jakuchū draws attention to the hydrangeas by placing them asymmetrically against starkly empty, shallow space. He makes the viewer dwell upon their intricacy and luminous color by engaging and guiding the eye, through rhythmic placement of flower clusters and birds. In his genius, Jakuchū combines technical virtuosity and psychological perception with a profound understanding of nature to create an air of serenity and animate presence.

The sharp contrast between the backgrounds and work of Brueghel and

Rooster, Hen and Hydrangeas by Itō Jakuchū
(L.83.50.1, eighteenth century), Etsuko and
Joe Price Collection, Corona del Mar.
Courtesy Los Angeles County Museum of Art.

Jakuchū shows us that there are many paths to success in floral design. Yet they have a common foundation in one irreplaceable thing: intimate knowledge of the flower itself. Each learned by reading the flower. Their works are masterpieces because in allowing the flower to guide them, their portrayals reveal its true spirit. By showing that individual style does not require sacrificing the beauty or character of the bloom, these artists left us a great gift. The flower does not know east, west, north, or south, but in its own quiet way, simply shares its perfection.

Contemporary Floral Design: Botanical to Abstract

Recognizing the different ways a composition engages us and incorporating this knowledge into design concepts are significant lessons. Eastern traditions teach us the role of well-developed theory in comprehending floral shape and form, and the absolute necessity of technique. They show us that if used as guides, rules perform critical functions by compelling us to read the flower and setting universal standards. When combined with the Western tradition's lively, spontaneous approach to color and, above all, avoidance of excessive formalism, we have a superb foundation for contemporary floral design, in which the flower—with its guiding principle of unity in "color," "form," and "function"—is the ultimate master of design.

These are exciting times. Flowers and plants from around the globe are available throughout the year. Within the framework of vase life, function, lifestyle, and architectural space, the creative options of contemporary design are unlimited, ranging from the almost botanical to the nearly abstract. Where a particular composition stands along that scale is only a matter of degree.

Abstraction is the defining quality of floral design. Even botanical compositions, which emphasize the specific identities of the plant material involved, contain an element of abstraction. Simply taking a bloom out of its original environment dilutes its botanical purity, which is why a floral design can never completely duplicate nature. As abstraction increases, inherent qualities of shape, form, or color, independent of floral identity, come forward. Yet a design can never be purely abstract because its foundation is a living flower. It is dangerous to alter the basic character of a bloom, to change it into something it is not, whether forcing it to mimic a material, a shape, or an animal. Such a conception loses the identity of the flower and brings into question both function and inspiration. Success can only come to those who take the time to read the flower and benefit from its incredible wisdom in design. Respect for the natural essence and character of our medium assures its identity will be preserved, even in abstract compositions.

A striking painting by Itō Jakuen, a follower of Itō Jakuchū, shows that when abstraction pays homage to nature as the master of pure expression, the result is not only aesthetically pleasing but also wonderfully adaptable. *Banana Leaves* would be just as at home in a contemporary Western environment as it was in the Eastern one for which it was painted: elegant simplicity gives it timeless beauty. Employing only neutral ink tones of black and gray, Jakuen depicts the plant at such close range that we see it only in part, in sharp relief against flat empty space. By making us dwell selectively upon the expressive qualities of pure shapes, Jakuen elevates the humble banana leaf to abstract art. He takes pleasure in the formal geometric beauty inherent in the natural condition of each leaf, including its tears and holes, and with them builds a composition based on the circle, rectangle, line, and arc. He does not include artificial elements, nor does he distort his subject by interfering with its natural shape or life cycle. Inspired to communicate what he read, Jakuen allowed nature to speak.

Effects of Color and Light

In Chapter One, we had lessons in the fundamental aesthetics of nature's art from the magnolia. These concepts aid us in the transition of the flower from its place in nature to its role in floral design.

Just as with fragrance, flowers are acutely sensitive to each other when it comes to color. Those we think might combine, when seen in the market or in the garden, may surprise us with their contrary natures in the vase. Some that seem destined for a hateful relationship may turn out to be the best of friends. Is that blos-

Banana Leaves by Itō Jakuen (L.83.50.16, late eighteenth–early nineteenth century), Etsuko and Joe Price Collection, Corona del Mar. Courtesy Los Angeles County Museum of Art.

The color wheel.

som pink? Or is it orange? By developing an instinct for how floral colors interact and applying this skill when composing, the designer gains considerable control over the final result of a floral design.

THE COLOR WHEEL

Nature has its own way of dealing with color, but we need a systematic way of describing what it presents. Just as borrowing the terminology for design elements and principles helped us to understand nature's methods of organization, applying standard artistic vocabulary and concepts for color will clarify for us nature's way with this crucial element. For this purpose, the color wheel remains unsurpassed.

The essential unit of color is a hue. Hue is color at peak intensity. Generally, we recognize three types: primary, secondary, and tertiary. A primary hue is a pure color, one that cannot be reduced in any way. Yellow, red, and blue are the only primary hues. A secondary hue consists of equal parts of two primaries; the three secondary hues are orange (yellow and red), green (yellow and blue), and violet (blue and red). Mixing one primary with one secondary creates a tertiary hue, of which there are six: red-orange, yellow-orange, yellow-green, blue-green, blue-violet, and red-violet. This basic group of twelve hues can be divided into infinite gradations. The complete progression through the yellow, red, and blue families produces the color wheel's distinctive circle.

Any single hue possesses three color variations: tint, tone, and shade. A tint results from the addition of white. Mixing with gray produces a tone. Using black instead creates a shade. On the color wheel these relationships appear as concentric circles of increasing intensity, progressing from pale tints in the outer ring, to pure hues, to grayed tones, and finally to dark shades in the center. The standard color wheel takes each of the twelve basic hues through its advance from tint to shade, but any color can be identified with one of these four terms.

Complementary hues, red and green, for example, appear opposite each other on the color wheel. Split complements appear to either side of a color's complement, as shown in the second color wheel. A triad is made up of three colors that are equal in value.

COLOR RELATIONSHIPS IN FLOWERS

When it comes to instruction upon the fascinating subject of floral hue, rarely do we encounter a more amenable bloom than the cheerful gerbera, whose appealing daisy shapes and inexhaustible variations call to mind round paint samples. Gerberas have a great deal to say about color proportion, harmonies, complements, and visual perception. This beautiful crowd splashed against a woven willow screen (pages 68–69) brings the dry definitions of the color wheel to life. Instantly, we want to choose a favorite and begin our journey with color.

Appearing in pure red, intense yellow, and a spectrum of secondary and tertiary colors in between, these gerberas show that even the exclusion of the blue color family can hardly be considered a limitation. The red and yellow families shown here illustrate specific types of color relationships and proportion: the cluster on the right comes entirely from the red range on the color wheel, demonstrating the concept of monochromatic harmony; the group on the left emphasizes the yellow side of the gerbera's spectrum, but the inclusion of blooms of red and shades of peach, adjacent to yellow on the color wheel, creates an analogous harmony. The peach-orange blooms on both sides are of particular note. As secondary and tertiary colors, they identify with both the red- and yellow-dominated groups. Just as important, they demonstrate how nearby colors interact. Mingling in strongly red combinations brings out their redness; where yellow dominates, they seem more peachy in hue.

When massed, gerberas vividly demonstrate basic color wheel concepts; read as individuals, they show that nature throws some of its standard assumptions out the window. The color wheel presents color simplistically, detached from any context. Nature, complex and always interacting with itself, does not conform to narrow man-made rules. Floral personality relies heavily on color, whether cool or warm, soft or intense, shades, tints, or pure. The visual quality of floral color changes according to the texture, thickness, translucency, or opacity of each petal or leaf. These natural nuances defy the artificial hues and reductive relationships of the color wheel. Changing floral color with spray paint or solution destroys these subtleties, making it more difficult to combine flowers. Relying upon a color wheel for color selection makes for more work and a less satisfactory result; natural colors are easier to use. Read a carefully selected bloom for guidance.

Each flower contains a lesson in color harmony and contrast. Consider the color relationship between a red gerbera bloom and its stem and foliage. Their complementary hues oppose one another, visually pulling apart. Nature makes frequent use of complementary color relationships, such as violet and yellow, where contrast may facilitate its aim in some way, but this does not apply to green.

Overleaf Gerberas on a willow screen. Flowers courtesy B & H Flowers, Carpenteria, California; screen courtesy Willow Mania, Pescadero, California.

The one universal color, green dominates the plant world. This makes it a unifier, one of nature's great neutrals. It fills the same role in floral design, because every flower retains its inborn affinity with the foliage and greens. It is why the green of the willow screen blends with all the gerberas regardless of their color, helping to unite the composition into a pleasing whole. When we consider complementary relationships in floral color, we must remove green from this role.

The nuances of natural color relationships become evident when we compare two gerberas with the same color petals but different centers of black or yellow-green. Regardless of the petal color, a bloom with a yellow-green center blends easily into a composition because the center is monochromatically harmonious with any surrounding greens. This makes the bloom itself more amenable with respect to companions. A black center completely changes the effect of the flower. It contrasts with the foliage and with the color of the bloom itself, creating a far more complex interplay of color and shape by calling attention to the differences of each part. Any black-centered flower must be considered as a nearly independent actor in a design. The broader lesson here is that in any composition, each part of every flower plays an active role.

COMBINING FLOWERS WITH TEXTILES

This wreath of freeze-dried roses and orange peel expands upon the gerbera's basic lesson on color relationships. Its peach, pink, and orange color combination breaks conventional rules of harmony in floristry, but a close reading of the roses shows that nature does not limit itself in this way. The roses are delicately colored with tints from the red family, from deep blush pink to the orange cast of peach, blending to creamy white at the very base of each petal. A range of color selections in any of these hues would make a beautiful harmony of subtle blendings and contrasts.

A designer is limited only by which materials will work best with the overall purpose and setting of the design, yet even here the flower is the best guide to color selection in accents and accessories. These images show how the color effect of the rose wreath changes, depending on which ribbon is paired with it. The cognac-colored ribbon, in monochromatic harmony with the creamy bases of the rose petal interiors, highlights the orange slices by picking up their warm cast. The

Rose wreath with cognac ribbon.

greater proportion of orange- and yellow-based tints distinguishes them in relation to the dominant pinks and peaches of the surrounding petals, making a composition based on an idea of subdued contrast: the two related color families are in delicate analogous harmony. Replacing the cognac-colored ribbon with one woven from orange and pink threads completely alters the effect of the blooms. Because it contains both color families, the ribbon picks up both equally in the wreath, so that the entire composition of roses, oranges, and ribbon becomes an exploration of monochromatic harmony.

Textiles are integral to the concept when one is settling on a floral design for an interior space, a party, or a wedding. Their fiber, style, texture, color, and pattern make an important contribution to the ambience and offer another framework for creative inspiration. Even a single textile can lead the designer in almost any direction.

The photograph on page 74 shows material in a floral pattern of muted browns and pinks on an off-white background, which is used as a springboard for an array of blooms and leaves. These could, depending on their combination, suggest each of the four seasons. Led by the colors of the textile, a working palette is created with seasonal foliage and flowers in shades of pink, peach, white, and yellow. The season will be determined by which colors the designer chooses to emphasize, as well as by the emotional associations each viewer brings to the composition.

A wintry atmosphere can be evoked by a design based upon whiteness and coolness; blossoms in white or white tinged with pink could be used, together with eucalyptus and dusty miller, whose silvery quality gives a chilly feel to the soft underlying green. These colors harmonize with or complement the pinks of the patterned cloth. Adding dark brown leaves to the pale floral-foliage combination provides needed contrast and, with the pink-tinged flowers, links the composition to the cloth's color palette.

The fresh, reborn quality of spring is achieved by mixing the cheery faces of gerberas, sweet peas, and tiny roses among larger soft-toned or white blossoms, which blend with the pinks and yellows of the cloth pattern; foliage of bright yellow-green bordered with red suggests new growth. By deepening the colors to the stronger yellows, reds, and dark greens, the intensity of summer is sug-

Rose wreath with orange and pink ribbon.

gested. Replacing delicate white blossoms with more robustly textured leaves in hues of deep red and mottled gold brings to mind the crisp snap of autumn.

In short, the designer has great control over a composition's effect and can creatively adapt to the demands of special occasions and any architectural style or environment. Less attractive color combinations in the surroundings can be downplayed by drawing attention away from them, without clashing. By creating harmony between the occasion and the space, a designer's work becomes the focal point for both.

LIGHT AND FLORAL COLOR

How and why colors in an arrangement appear the way they do lies in the complex relationship between light and color. A basic understanding of this relationship is an extremely important aspect of floral design. Blooms may appear to be one color where we select them and another where we use them, depending on the time of day, their placement, and the type of light that illuminates them, a phenomenon known as color shift. Perceived object color is of utmost concern to designers. Even if the variant conditions that affect it are understood, it may still be necessary to consult a lighting specialist for permanent lighting applications.

All light has color of its own, which occurs across a spectrum ranging from warm to cool in hue. Any one type of light originates from a point along that spectrum. This point is its color temperature. Color temperature, which refers only to the light itself, is measured according to the Kelvin scale, or degrees K. This system has no relation to atmospheric measures of environmental warmth, like Fahrenheit and Celsius, in which higher temperature means greater heat; in the Kelvin scale, the higher the degrees K, the cooler the light. Even though we think of red as a warm color and blue as a cool one, a light originating from a blue point in the spectrum is brighter and has a higher color temperature than one from a red point in the spectrum. Daylight ranges from 5000K to 7500K. This natural light, to which our eyes are so conditioned, is a cool one that flatters flowers of blue and violet. A typical incandescent lightbulb produces a light of around 3000K, while the light of a candle measures 2000K. Blues look dull under such warm color temperatures, but reds and yellows appear vibrant. For this reason, when

Combining flowers with textiles.

1

2

3

4

5

6

planning an arrangement that will be displayed in artificial light, the designer should always note the degrees к of the light source, indicated on each lightbulb.

This series of six photographs demonstrates the degree to which light can alter our perception of floral color. Each features an arrangement of gerberas, violets, allium, and delphinium in one of the various environments a designer commonly encounters. A camera does not see in quite the same way as a human eye sees, so what it records can only approximate direct experience; moreover, the designer should always keep in mind that actual conditions can be very changeable, and that a room may be illuminated by several different types of light at once. In conveying the subtle changes of hue that can occur, these images nevertheless introduce the basics of the special challenge that lighting presents.

The first three photographs show the arrangement in one location under conditions typical of a home: by a window in daylight, under incandescent light, and by candlelight. The delphinium, vibrantly blue under daylight, acquires a reddish cast in incandescent light and becomes a nearly saturated violet in candlelight. The allium ranges in color from bluish pink in daylight to deep red-pink in candlelight. The pale yellow gerbera that appears nearly white under the cool daylight intensifies in the warmth of the incandescent light and candlelight, while the bright yellow one acquires an increasingly brassy coloration as the color temperature decreases. The pale pink gerbera gradually becomes peachier in tone; the two red gerberas and the multicolored pink gerbera become deeper.

The next three show the same flowers in the controlled environment of a light booth. This replicates the artificial light conditions of offices, particularly those without windows. In these more sterile situations, light will be more consistent and predictable but also more harsh. The first photograph displays the arrangement under a fluorescent adjusted for daylight at 5000k. The next shows them beneath a typical office fluorescent at 3500k; the purples look dull here. Their vibrance in the 5000k fluorescent is due to the proximity of violet to ultraviolet

1. Daylight in a home.
2. Incandescent light in a home.
3. Candlelight in a home.
4. Fluorescent light adjusted for daylight at 5000K.
5. Fluorescent light at 3500K.
6. Incandescent light at 2700K.

in the spectrum, which is how sunlight renders color; this makes all the reds and purples take on a more bluish cast. The gerbera that appears pale salmon-pink under typical fluorescent at 3500K is a clear pink in the light adjusted for daylight. Both types of fluorescent give yellows a deeper coloration. In the final photograph, ordinary home incandescent at 2700K, pink and red look warm and luscious, and the gerberas now appear bright yellow.

In short, blue and violet flowers that look lively and distinct in daylight will appear duller when exposed to artificial light with a cooler color temperature. Hues in the red and yellow families appear the most vivid. Note that in all cases, white does not take on the actual coloration of the light, but its brightness recedes as temperature decreases. Overall, as the temperature declines and the light takes on a warmer coloration, hues beneath it both deepen and blend. This is not only because lower intensity light is less bright: the neutralizing effect of the increasingly red quality of the light is also at work.

In addition to color temperature in degrees Kelvin, light is also measured according to the Color Rendering Index, or CRI, which rates (on a scale of 0 to 100) each light source for the amount of color it emits at its particular color temperature. Natural daylight has a CRI of 70. Incandescent light has a CRI near 100, and the best fluorescent light a CRI of 82. Most artificial light sources will indicate a CRI score in addition to the degrees K. But be warned: each lightbulb is manufactured a little differently, and two lightbulbs with the same color temperature may not have identical ranges of color. Knowing that these factors exist will sharpen your sensitivity to color selection and visual perception in artificially lit environments.

Considering the Container

The container plays an active role in a design and, like all elements, must be understood in terms of color, form, and function. In addition to its practical role as the primary water source, its appearance and size influence the final outcome of a composition. It can be barely visible, simply there to provide water and give flowers and greens just enough lift to let them dance, a method used mostly for low centerpieces. It can be a neutral presence, blending seamlessly with foliage and background colors, or a safe approach, such as clear glass. Or—most challenging and enjoyable—it can be the visual link between the flowers and their surroundings. In general, unless a deliberate effect of contrast is desired, the container's intrinsic qualities of color, texture, size, style, and mood should harmonize with the blooms and the space they occupy, making the total composition more than the sum of its parts.

In matching containers to the flowers, setting, and each other, designers and clients alike delight in exercising their creative flair. Interesting combinations emerge when you look beyond obvious associations of style or era and let yourself be inspired by shape, color, and spirit. In the group assembled on page 80, the exquisite green vases of handblown Murano glass, a well-designed clear glass cylinder, and a wine glass share characteristics of material and simple, clean shape. The green of the vases blends in analogous harmony with the blue snake winding down the stem of the wine glass; the snake in turn pulls the antique porcelain Chinese ginger jars into the group by harmonizing with their blue and white pattern. They in turn complement the shape, color, and material of the two contemporary ceramic vases. The gold-leafed bamboo-shaped vase picks up the spirit of the Chinese jars, while its bright metallic gleam points to a gift from my favorite uncle: a well-used copper bread-dough pot from Holland, whose warm coloration blends nicely with the yellow highlights of the Murano vases, completing the circle. The pewter candlestick—a seeming oddball at first glance—harmonizes with the blue and white with its cool color, and the metals and glass with its soft sheen.

Clear glass is a marvelously versatile neutral. It disappears even as it illuminates everything it contains, so that the entire floral stem plus supporting materials become part of the design. With glass, we do not need a large budget to have good containers; even a wine or mineral water bottle will do to begin a collection. The industry has come out with a large selection of well-designed vases suitable for personal and professional needs. The three smallest grouped in the photograph on page 81 are good examples. Their relatively narrow openings and wide interiors allow for easy placement of many kinds of stems, and their classic shape adapts to many situations. Arrangements in such containers would be appropriate as small hospitality gifts, as individual place settings, or, as shown on pages 172–173 of the Gallery, as a celebration of new life. To maintain the pristine clarity necessary for designs in clear glass, use two identical vases; make your design in one and transfer it to the other, with clean water, before delivery or display.

Overleaf, left Green Murano glass and other containers. Styling by Douglas Sandberg.

Overleaf, right Clear glass and other containers. Styling by Milena Boucher.

The group of containers opposite shows that—East or West, antique or contemporary—materials of all kinds can mingle with style. A designer who knows how to combine containers can create arresting displays in the shop and personalize work for clients. At home, it is hard to come by the lengthy hours needed to accomplish certain floral designs; happily, the joy of a lovely composition is easily had, with only a single stem in a handsome or intriguing container. A simple arrangement of stems in favorite containers, offset by a slender candle and gifts that remind you of dear ones, can be even more special to come home to than a massive display of many flowers.

Globalization and readily available mechanical aids have brought unlimited possibility to what we use as holders for flowers. Yet some of the most clever ideas may arise from a stroll in a farmers market or a walk on the beach. Gourds and other vegetables, fruits, driftwood, and other unusual items make appealing containers when drilled with a cavity and fitted with a glass test tube or cylinder. A few self-adhesive acrylic pads (such as Bump-ONs, a 3M product) on the bottom will stabilize the unorthodox vessel and add surface protection. As the examples on pages 150–151 and 217 of the Gallery demonstrate, these amusing treatments can stand alone or combine with typical vases, transforming an ordinary composition into one of wit and unconventionality.

Used to advantage, containers are wonderful assets that can make a statement even as they highlight the natural quality of the blooms. As long as the container's intrinsic qualities accord with the design concept, assembly will be easy to accomplish and the relationship mutually enhancing. Gleaming metal and sparkling cut glass enhance flowers of simple shape and clear color. Their more subtle cousins' complexities of hue and texture play in exquisite concert with the lustrous deep glazes of pottery and the patinas of bronze and other metals. The color and character of many natural materials, such as terra cotta, wood, and simple but good basketry, complement a large array of flowers in informal settings.

Gourds and other unexpected items can be transformed into containers when drilled and fitted with glass cylinders and stabilized with self-adhesive acrylic pads.

Opposite Japanese plate and other containers.
Styling by Jacqueline Hermann.

The shape of a container influences the number of flowers it can hold and how those flowers will behave in it. Narrow-mouthed containers, easiest for arranging flowers and holding them in place, accommodate relatively few stems. Cylinders, which tend to hold stems in upright positions, can also be stunning for flowers that trail and arch. A cylinder's width at the bottom, in addition to its weight, will determine the length of the flowers you can safely use. Wide-mouthed containers are wonderful for holding flowers in quantity but may need a means to secure their contents. Shallow containers require an enhancing water source, such as floral foam.

The choice of container is part of the creative process and often opens the door to a lovely design. Picture your own selection from the array shown in this section, and look to the Gallery for more ideas. Only our imaginations can limit what we dream up as a container and how we use it.

The practical challenges associated with the container and the other lessons presented in this chapter, from the worlds of history, art, aesthetics, and science, may seem overwhelming. But they are important ones, for they enrich our understanding of the flower. When the time comes to begin, step back and relax. Let the blooms be your guide in their placement—allow them to speak.

CHAPTER THREE

Working with Flowers

One good look at a flower shows not only nature's incredible beauty but also its absolute brilliance in design, from general construction to the smallest detail. With every element serving a precise purpose, the exquisitely utilitarian flower teaches us that we too must be mindful of floral care and adhere to good construction and design techniques, to do our medium justice. A well-planned and well-made design cannot help but bring out its beauty.

Floral Care

Obtaining your flowers is the first step in floral design. To secure a good product, purchase flowers from a reputable grower, wholesaler, or florist. Look for firm petals that are not bruised or otherwise damaged. Colors should be clear. Foliage and stems should look healthy and be free of decay. Garden cuttings should be taken in the early morning, when all water loss is replenished. Second choice is late in the afternoon. Garden flowers do best if they are placed in tepid water directly after they are cut.

The second step is to condition your flowers by processing and hardening them; this prolongs the life of the bloom by maximizing water intake and minimizing bacterial growth. To further retard the growth of bacteria, keep both storage buckets and tools very clean, and mix the water in which the blooms will be

Muscari latifolium (grape hyacinth).

stored with one-quarter teaspoon of household bleach or floral preservative per gallon. To facilitate absorption, use tepid water, which contains the least amount of air; an air bubble can block the vascular system of a stem. Using either a sharp knife or scissors, recut your materials under water, on a long diagonal slant, to provide a large area for water intake. Remove any foliage below the water level, to discourage the growth of bacteria. Woody stems should be cut with sharp clippers and given a vertical slit. Flower stems that exude latex, a milky substance, should be seared in boiling water after they are cut in order to seal them. Do not recut after searing.

Keep your flowers in a cool area, away from drafts and direct sunlight, to harden for at least two hours. They can then be transferred to a floral refrigerator. For a majority of flowers, floral refrigerators should be kept at 40F. Orchids and other tropical blooms and foliage are best maintained at 55–60F, with the temperature never dipping below 50F. In all cases, relative humidity should be maintained at 50–80 percent. In unavoidable conditions of warmth and low humidity, spray leaves and stems after prep, allow them to dry, and cover loosely with a sheet of thin plastic (dry cleaning bags are excellent for this purpose) before refrigerating. The plastic acts like a greenhouse to keep moisture levels high. Low humidity will wilt flowers faster than warm temperatures.

A water quality analysis can provide the professional florist with important information about the municipal water supply's acidity, as well as its fluoride, mineral salt, and alkaline content. If you are a professional, you can enhance longevity by educating your clients. Include a floral care tag with completed designs.

Materials for floral design: wire wreath forms, raffia, electrical ties, self-adhesive acrylic pads, sharp knives, bamboo saw, plexiglass rod, bamboo, curly willow, red-stemmed dogwood, mosses and lichens (from top to bottom: Spanish moss, Iceland moss, lichen, sphagnum moss, Sierra lichen, mood moss, sheet moss), assembled extender, funeral cone, decorative stones, twine, branch clippers, clear floral tape, green floral tape, and flower scissors.

For more information, refer to the Society of American Florists's *Flower and Plant Care Manual* and the excellent booklet on the care of individual flowers published by Ikebana International (see "Plant and Flower Identification and Care" in Suggested Reading).

Construction: Materials and Techniques

FLORAL FOAM

Because it is easy to use and transport, providing stability and an adequate water source, floral foam is used by many professional designers. Smithers-Oasis is the best-known brand.

All floral foam saturates best when floated in warm water that has first been treated with one-quarter teaspoon of bleach or preservative per gallon. Float the floral foam with the punctured air hole facing down, and allow it to absorb at its own rate; pressing it down will only cause it to trap air. Instant De Luxe bricks will saturate within five minutes; designer blocks may take up to thirty minutes. Floral foam does not expand as it saturates. It can be cut to size either before or after soaking.

For low-rimmed containers, floral foam provides not only an adequate water source but also good stem support. After soaking, join the pieces of floral foam together using bamboo skewers. Cut the floral foam to a size that will allow each stem to be inserted at least three inches into it; leave a margin between it and the inside of the container, for a water source, and cover of sheet moss. Use clear floral tape to secure the floral foam and moss in the container. This will provide enough support for most small to medium designs.

Opposite More materials for floral design: liners, adhesive, leaf gloss (such as Leafshine, a Pokon product), spray and water bottles, chicken wire, and floral foam in various shapes and sizes (wreaths, igloo cage, funeral cage, designer block, regular brick, grande block).

Tray and vase with floral foam cut to fit.

For round vases, especially if a great number of stems are going to be used, it is best to cut a cylinder that closely fits the mouth of the container. Depending on the size of the container and number of flowers to be used, the floral foam should extend at least one to four inches above the rim. Cut a wedge in the cylinder for adding and maintaining a water supply.

LARGE CONSTRUCTIONS AND EXTENDERS

Large-scale architectural spaces, such as church sanctuaries, country clubs, and hotel lobbies, often have large containers in place. These require liners, which means that the construction of the short-term work that so frequently graces such spaces, such as designs for weddings and parties, can be accomplished in the studio or shop and then easily transported to the site.

The foundation for large arrangements (see pages 189 and 191 of the Gallery) begins with a papier-mâché liner into which dry floral foam is placed. Both designer and grande blocks fill the liner and extend well above its rim. In this way, stems can later be inserted along the sides. The top is covered with chicken wire and anchored firmly in place with waterproof tape. The entire construction is next soaked upside down in lukewarm water for around thirty minutes. It is then removed from the water and covered with sheet moss.

Floral designs for large architectural spaces sometimes require more height than the flower stem can provide. Extenders constructed from funnels solve this problem. The exterior of the funnel is first hidden by gluing sheet moss around it, rendering it almost invisible in a completed design.

Cut two equal lengths of bamboo, leaving the side branches on. Insert the nail that extends from the bottom of the funnel into the open end of one bamboo, using glue to secure it. Place the second length of bamboo beside the first, and wire and moss them together in one or two places. Pull the side branches along the sides of the funnel, and wire and glue them around it. Cut a block of soaked floral foam to fit, filling the funnel up to about one inch below the rim. Cover the top with moss, fitting it inside the funnel.

This type of extender can be placed into the base on site. It should be inserted deeply, nearly to the bottom of the liner. The chicken wire holding the floral foam and liner together also gives the extenders extra support. Several extenders may be used, their height varying according to the needs of the space.

Bamboo extenders in papier-mâché liner.

ALTERNATIVE CONSTRUCTION

Beautiful supports that become part of the design can be constructed with branches. In this photograph, a tepee-like structure of red-stemmed dogwood (*Cornus* spp.) is held together with an electrical tie, and green curly willow (*Salix* spp.) bends easily into an armature that will both support flowers and become part of the design. Other types of branches may also be used, but beware of swelling from water immersion, and, if using a glass container, take care not to apply too much pressure as you wedge the branches in, as this can break the glass.

A grid made from clear floral tape provides a clean and nearly invisible support system. Tape around the rim of the container as well, to secure the grid. Grids made from tape give good support and will hold the flowers in place if water needs replacing before delivery. They are especially useful for wedding and party work. A loose ball of chicken wire also gives excellent support—but should be used only in opaque containers.

Four different floral supports. Containers courtesy
Floral Supply Syndicate, San Francisco Flower Mart.

A wire wreath form and curly willow provide a double support system in this copper pot—a beautiful alternative to floral foam for designs requiring many flowers in fresh water. The first set of branches is woven through the wreath, extending over the edge of the container to create a stable work grid; the arching branches at top are secured inside the bowl and can become part of the design.

PLANTS AND ALTERNATIVE CONTAINERS

Liners come in a wide range of sizes and shapes. Combined with the use of floral foam as a time-released water source under and around plants, they enable the designer to make use of alternative containers and whole plants instead of cut flowers. The result of the wonderful flexibility they provide is longer-lasting

Copper pot with wire wreath form and curly willow.

designs that require minimal care (see the azalea display on page 161 of the Gallery).

As a planter, this large aluminum platter relies for its appeal upon the contrast between its flat metallic sheen and the lovely texture of club moss (*Selaginella* spp.). To assemble, place dry floral foam on the bottom to provide a secure, level foundation extending to the rim of the platter. Place two rectangular liners on top. Remove eighteen selaginella mosses from their pots and arrange them in three rows of three in each liner. Fill the gaps between them with pieces of dry floral foam, and water your design. The floral foam helps to stabilize the construction, making it as practical as it is flexible. It can be maintained for weeks with minimal care. This design is also adaptable. It can be augmented with the addition of short-

Mechanics for selaginella moss planter.

To celebrate spring, nothing can surpass bulbs, as this grand display of potted yellow 'Hella Light' tulips at Filoli clearly shows. Styling by Lucy Tolmach.

lived cut flowers, such as violets, for a completely different mood. See pages 158 and 159 of the Gallery.

Plants and Bulbs in Floral Design

In addition to its role in landscaping; as a container plant, potted for inside and outside use; and as a cut flower in floral designs, the bulb plant—so beautiful from the top all the way down to its roots—invites creative fun during its bud–to–bloom stages. A hyacinth, narcissus, miniature iris, or a botanical tulipa, with its enticing interplay of texture, color, shape, and form, can make a complete statement when placed singly in a small container or even a wine glass. Used alone or grouped, they create striking contemporary settings.

Pot of paperwhite narcissus (*Narcissus papyraceus*) and mechanics.

Paperwhite narcissus in glass.

Keeping the whole plant intact highlights the head-to-toe beauty of bulb flowers and prolongs the time they can be displayed. The bulb is an amazing package that provides nourishment to the flower it produces. It needs no soil to bloom and can be maintained easily with an adequate water source and misting in low humidity. Before they are used, the bulb and its roots should be thoroughly washed of any soil. Wrap the roots into a pretty nest before placing in a container. (The roots can be trimmed, but remember that cut edges will turn brown.) Swizzle sticks, skewers, black or green bamboo, red-stemmed dogwood, or curly willow can be used as support structures.

Big bulbs, such as amaryllis, are dramatic in individual containers that complement the shape of the bulb. This composition is designed to highlight the brilliant red of the bloom. The neutral color of the bowl, stones, and black bamboo support blend with the hue of the bulb. With the stem and flower head discreetly supported with a tie such as gold thread or brass wire, an elegant statement results.

Amaryllis (*Hippeastrum* spp.) in a bowl.

This design demonstrates a lovely way to take full advantage of groups of small bulbs. A composition of neutrals, the mottled gray-green of the stones supporting the bulbs blends nicely with the brighter green of the foliage of both the bulbs and the lily grass (*Liriope exiliflora*), which has been added for movement. The angularity of the stones is complemented by the square shape of the container. The geometry of these shapes is a welcome foil to the graceful arc of stems, leaves, and blooms. Because the design relies upon the transparency of the container for its effect, bulbs must be absolutely clean.

Freesias (*Freesia alba*) in glass.

When in bloom, quite a few orchids are amenable to being removed from their pots for more attractive display. Armatures of willow, dogwood, bamboo, or manzanita bring striking beauty to orchid arrangements and are also highly practical. Carefully packing the plant roots with sphagnum moss provides an excellent moisture source. Sheet moss or fresh Spanish lichen is indispensable for attractive camouflage and finishing. Designs employing this technique can last for weeks with little or no attention. This makes them ideal for situations like conventions or trade shows, where high-maintenance designs would require extra staffing and interfere with public activity. For a variation on this technique, see how dendrobiums and oncidiums are used with woven armatures of manzanita on pages 164–165 and 166–167 of the Gallery.

Moth orchids (*Phalaenopsis* spp.) in ginger pots.

Design: Materials and Techniques

WIRING AND TAPING TECHNIQUES

The wiring and taping of flowers and leaves is called for only when extra support is needed for the design to function. It should be kept to a minimum and done so that it detracts as little as possible from the natural beauty of the plant materials. The following examples are useful techniques, many of which can be used in arrangements, corsages, or wedding bouquets. Enameled wires, 18-gauge (heaviest) to 28-gauge (thinnest) in twelve- or eighteen-inch lengths, are used for various degrees of support. Heavy flowers or those with long stems usually need a lower-gauge wire, while lighter-weight flowers usually require a higher-gauge wire. These are the factors to consider while choosing the appropriate wire gauge: the function of the flower and the length of the flower stem within the design.

For roses and other solid-stemmed flowers, wrap an 18-gauge wire with tape beginning a half-inch from one end. Lay wire next to the stem, and insert the bare half-inch of the wire into the calyx, or base of the flower. Tape the wire to the stem in one or two places. This technique provides good support, leaves the natural stem visible, and permits the foliage (if any) to remain.

Flowers with a hollow stem can be supported by the insertion of a wire up the hollow channel of the stem and into the base of the flower.

Tulips, the only flowers that grow after being cut, may need a special armature of wire to support and control the direction of the stem, which adds three to four inches during the vase life of the flower. Wrap an 18-gauge wire with tape. Take one end of the wire and twist it into a small loop, around the lower end of the tulip stem. Slide the loop of the lower stem, and widen it slightly to form a collar that will fit loosely around the upper stem, just below the flower head. With the

Materials for wiring and taping: spool wire, light green floral tape, corsage and boutonniere pins, cotton balls, ribbon, wire in various sizes and lengths, wire cutters, wire gauge, floral preservative or sealer, ribbon scissors, knife, spray bottle, low-heat glue gun, glue sticks, clear floral adhesive tape, corsage stems, rose corsage stems, paper towels, boutonniere bags, corsage bags, thin plastic bags.

collar in place, lay the length of the taped wire next to the stem. Tape the wire to the stem in one or two places (see photograph).

For flowers to be used in small hand-tied bouquets, a thin wire of 26- or 28-gauge will provide enough support for the stem and flower, while minimizing the weight of the bouquet and bulk of the handle.

Tender-stemmed flowers, such as lily of the valley (*Convallaria majalis*), benefit from a narrow strip of paper towel wrapped around the approximate area of the binding point. This provides protection from damage during construction of a hand-tied bouquet. Tape any portion of the paper strip on the stem that will be visible.

Wiring and taping roses, tulips, and other flowers.

Roses and other large- or heavy-stemmed flowers intended for corsages and weddings will generally require corsage stems or rose corsage stems, available from your local floral supplier. Soak these rose corsage stems for about five minutes in water. Cut the rose at the lower end of its calyx, matching the width of the corsage stem as closely as possible. Insert the wire tip of the rose corsage stem firmly into the calyx. Insert a cross wire (28-gauge) through the top of the calyx, bend it down on both sides, and wrap once around the corsage stem to make a support. (For flowers lacking a calyx or firm center, leave a half-inch length of the stem intact, and insert the tip of the corsage stem into it; cross wire.) Wrap with light green floral tape. Begin taping at the base of the calyx, progressing to the top of the calyx, forming a collar, before proceeding down the stem, stretching the tape gently for a tight, clean surface. Extra support wire can be added to extend the length, if necessary.

For the wiring and taping of leaves, the stitch technique provides a good support. Take the leaf in your hand, back side up and stem toward you. Half to one-third up from the base of the leaf, stitch a wire (the gauge depending on the size of the leaf and the amount of support required) horizontally through the midrib. (Only a small stitch will be visible on the front of the leaf.) Hold the leaf at the stitch point firmly on both sides, between your thumb and index finger, to minimize damage to the leaf. With the other hand, bend both wire ends down at once toward the stem of the leaf. Wrap once or twice around the stem. For corsage work, taping and cotton may be necessary. If taping is needed, do not wrap wire around the stem, but lay it on each side of the stem. To tape, begin about one-half inch below the leaf, proceeding up to the base, and then go down after forming a nice collar, stretching gently as you go to make a smooth, tight finish. This technique is not only attractive but is also secure, and will not come off or loosen.

HAND-TIED TECHNIQUES

Techniques for hand-tied bouquets are simple, but repeated practice is necessary to do them well. Once you have mastered the requisite precision and eye-hand coordination, you will be rewarded with versatile and polished presentations. The key to a successful hand-tied bouquet is the control of the binding point, or the point of union between the materials of the bouquet and the top of the handle or the container they occupy. For learning purposes, be sure to begin with materials that have sturdy stems; fragile or hollow stems are easily damaged if held or tied too tightly.

Hand-tied bouquets rely upon one or more types of materials to give the completed construction its form. Although they are sometimes used interchangeably, it will clarify things to apply the terms describing these materials in very specific ways. Single-flower stems (one bloom per stem) give impact and definition to a composition. Multiple-flower stems (many blooms on one stem) provide a natural grouping. Spreaders are clustered foliage, berries, or inflorescences of small blooms, such as hydrangeas, that create volume. Fillers are soft greens and inflorescences of small blooms that create airiness. Finishers are leaves or vines that create an attractive and protective frame at the base of the bouquet.

Plan your bouquet carefully, according to its intended purpose and ultimate surroundings. For color, take your cue from one flower, allowing its harmonies and complements to guide the rest of your selection. Consider how the relation-

ship of the size, shape, and behavior of individual materials will affect the ultimate appearance of the bouquet.

Spiral technique for vase and presentation bouquets

The color scheme of this composition is based upon the Ecuadorian and floribunda spray roses, whose subtle range of dusky peaches and pinks makes a beautiful union with the autumnal red-browns of the hydrangea leaves. The pink hydrangeas combine with the lilies and roses; the green ones blend with the soft yet bright greens of the pittosporum, bringing liveliness and spark. The rich dark pink of the sumac inflorescences heralds the introduction of the stargazer lilies, whose clear bright pinks soften and deepen in this mixture of quieter hues. The dark green and brown-red galax leaves make a frame that both harmonizes and defines.

Materials for presentation bouquet, spiral technique. Single-flower stems: Ecuadorian roses in deep dusky pinks and peaches. Multiple-flower stems: stargazer lilies in white with pink, floribunda spray roses in pink, peach, and cream. Spreaders: hydrangeas in pink and soft green with red-brown autumn leaves. Fillers: miniature variegated pittosporum, sumac (*Rhus* spp.). Finisher: galax leaves in deep brown-red and green.

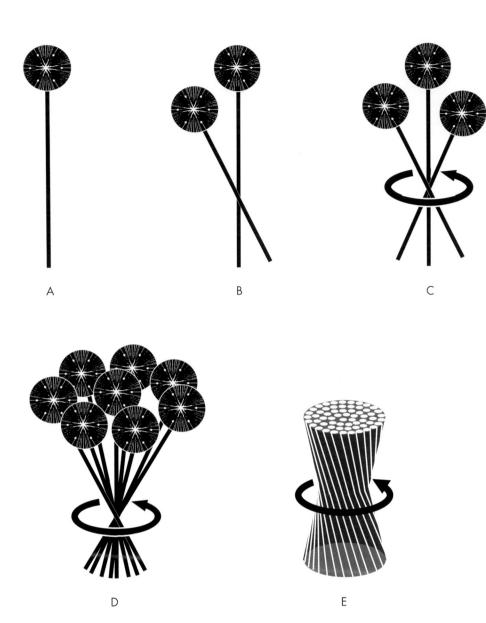

A

B

C

D

E

Spiral binding technique,
Diagrams A, B, C, D, and E.

To assemble your presentation bouquet:

Step 1. Select flowers and greens.

Step 2. Choose an approximate height and width for the completed bouquet, based upon the quantity and size of your flowers (and, for vase bouquets, the size of the container). This determines the binding point.

Step 3. Lay materials out on a work table. Remove all foliage from the stems below the approximate binding point. Wire flowers for support, if necessary.

Step 4. Select your central flower. When first learning this technique, it is helpful to tie a small ribbon just below the flower head of this stem, to make it easy to keep track of the center of the bouquet. (Diagram A.)

Step 5. Hold the central flower in front of you at the binding point, between the thumb and index finger of your weaker hand (for most people, this will be the left hand). Take your next flower, look at it, and, pointing the stem away from you, place it to the left of the main flower. Their stems should cross at the binding point. (Diagram B.)

Step 6. Continue laying flowers in this fashion, stem pointing away and flower head facing you. Place each next to the one that preceded it, regularly turning the bouquet one-quarter turn, incorporating spreaders or fillers as necessary. Use your stronger hand to assist. In this way, a spiral of stems begins to form. At first, your bouquet will not feel stable; it will become increasingly secure, however, as you add flowers and greens. As the bouquet grows, use the area between your thumb and index finger to hold it like a collar; this will give the muscles of your thumb and finger a chance to relax. (Diagrams C, D, and E.)

Step 7. Check often to make sure that your central flower remains in the center of the bouquet.

Step 8. When the bouquet is as large as you intend it to be, finish it with leaves, vines, or branches.

Step 9. Tie the bouquet at the binding point with raffia, twine, or ribbon. It should be tight enough to keep the bouquet together, but not so tight as to damage the stems.

Step 10. Cut the stems to the same length. Your bouquet should be able to stand on its own on a flat surface. Recut the stems before placing the completed bouquet in water.

Overleaf, left Hand-tied presentation bouquet, spiral technique, tied with ribbon.

Overleaf, right Completed presentation bouquet from above.

The presentation bouquet at intended size.

The bouquet should be able to stand on a flat surface.

Spiral technique for wedding bouquets

The secret for success in wedding bouquets, whether intended for the bride, her mother, or her attendants, is twofold. First, materials must be in top condition and fully hardened, because unlike a container design, they must be strong enough to hold up in the absence of an ample water source. Second, the bouquet's form must remain open when the stems below the binding point are pulled together to form a handle. Because the bridesmaid's bouquet we are about to assemble needs to be small, spherical, and only slightly open, it employs multiple-flower stems as spreaders, fillers, and finishers to complete its form.

Likewise taking its cue from the Ecuadorian roses, this composition's color scheme is urged to a brighter, softer cast of coloration than the presentation bouquet we just completed. Floribunda spray roses in a mixture of colors including peach, soft pink, and ivory are added to blend with the brighter pink of the hydrangeas. Together with the ranunculus, which occur in a range of pink tints, the floribunda spray roses function as transitions among the other flowers.

Materials for bridesmaid's bouquet, spiral technique. Single-flower stems: Ecuadorian roses in dusky pink; ranunculus in a range of pink tints. Spreaders, fillers, and finishers: floribunda spray roses in peach and ivory; hydrangeas in pink colors.

To assemble your bridesmaid's bouquet:

Step 1. Lay materials out on a work table. Remove all foliage from the stems below the approximate binding point. Wire where necessary, using 28-gauge wire. This gauge provides gentle support and is easy to trim as you form the handle. Replace the heavy stems of the Ecuadorian roses with rose corsage stems. (See "Wiring and Taping Techniques" earlier in this chapter.)

Step 2. As in the presentation bouquet, tie a small ribbon just below the head of the central flower, if needed, to make it easy to see. Begin laying on the flowers in the spiral method, turning regularly and using spreaders or fillers when needed.

Assembling bridesmaid's bouquet, Step 2.

Step 3. As you proceed, place the flowers at slightly different levels, creating a spherical form. You can control the form by using a mirror to see both sides of the design.

Assembling bridesmaid's bouquet, Step 3.

Step 4. Wire or tie the binding point, holding all the stems together. Trim stems where necessary to form a slender, tapering handle that complements the bouquet's size and scale. Mist the completed bouquet.

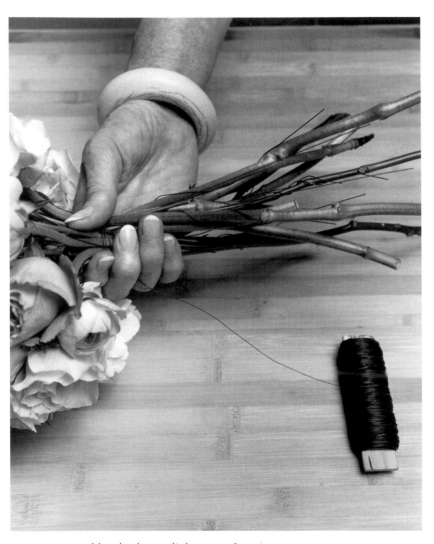

Assembling bridesmaid's bouquet, Step 4.

Step 5. Place the bouquet in water up to the binding point. When the misted flowers have dried, cover with thin plastic to keep in moisture, and place in a floral refrigerator or cool place. This bouquet can be made one or two days before the wedding and kept in water until the day of delivery.

Assembling bridesmaid's bouquet, Step 5.

To finish your bridesmaid's bouquet:

Step 1. Check to make sure all flowers and greens are in top condition. Replace where necessary.

Step 2. Check your handle to make sure no wires or stems protrude.

Step 3. Cut a paper towel to the length of the handle. Wrap it around the handle and spray with water.

Finishing bridesmaid's bouquet, Step 3.

Step 4. Using one-inch-wide green floral tape, wrap the handle, beginning from the bottom.

Step 5. Cut a small boutonniere bag to the length of the handle and slip it on, to maintain moisture in the bouquet and to prevent leakage.

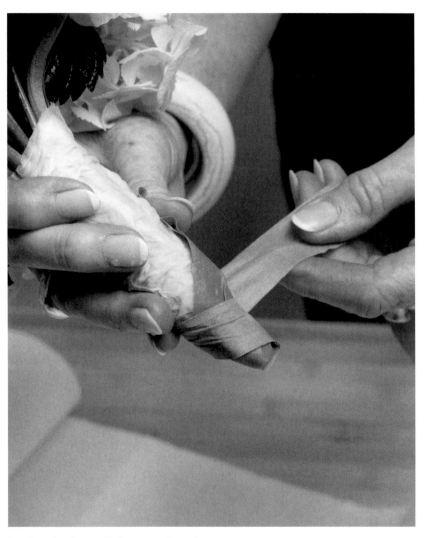

Finishing bridesmaid's bouquet, Step 4.

Step 6. Using one-inch-wide clear tape, wrap the handle, beginning from the bottom. Fold the boutonniere bag neatly against it as you go, making a construction that is secure and smooth.

Finishing bridesmaid's bouquet, Step 5.

Finishing bridesmaid's bouquet, Step 6.

Step 7. Spray the bouquet lightly with a floral preservative or sealer, such as Crowning Glory, to keep moisture in the flowers (do not use on fuzzy leaves or oil-based plant polish). Set the bouquet in an empty vase or glass to dry.

Finishing bridesmaid's bouquet, Step 7.

Step 8. Use a low-heat glue gun to attach a ribbon to the bouquet at the binding point, leaving a tail of sufficient length to later become part of the bow, and keep the rest of the ribbon on the roll.

Finishing bridesmaid's bouquet, Step 8.

Step 9. Glue the ribbon down the handle, to the tip end. Fold it neatly over the bottom, and glue on the sides of the handle to secure.

Step 10. Wrap ribbon carefully around the bottom of the handle, gluing it in place. Wind slowly and neatly up the handle, using glue on both handle and ribbon. This will secure the ribbon so that it cannot slide, even if the bouquet is carried all day.

Finishing bridesmaid's bouquet, Step 9.

Finishing bridesmaid's bouquet, Step 10.

Step 11. At the binding point, check mechanics of bouquet and handle for neatness. Again glue ribbon in place, and, before finally cutting ribbon off, pull a second length of ribbon from roll, enough to form the other side of the bow. Tie the two lengths into a bow. Secure the bow with glue or a corsage pin (or both). (Make sure any pins are used in such a way that they cannot harm the bearer.)

Step 12. Slip a boutonniere bag over the handle to protect it during storage. Cover once more with thin plastic. Refrigerate bouquet if necessary until delivery, making sure that the ribbon does not get wet.

Overleaf Completed bridesmaid's bouquet.

Finishing bridesmaid's bouquet, Step 11.

Straight-stem technique

Straight-stem hand-tied techniques are used for narrow vases, contemporary compositions, and small wedding bouquets. The composition shown on page 132, a playful pull between two primary colors, yellow and red, features the unusually tactile *Heliconia vellerigera,* the foliage and berries of heavenly bamboo (*Nandina domestica*), philodendron and variegated flax leaves, and persimmons (*Diospyros kaki*).

To assemble your straight-stem bouquet:

Step 1. Select your materials carefully, keeping in mind the key elements of color and form.

Step 2. Lay materials out on a work table. Remove all foliage from the stems below the approximate binding point.

Step 3. Select your central flower or flowers.

Step 4. Lay succeeding materials next to the central stems, exactly where you want them to appear in your design, either to the left, right, front, or back of the central flower. Do not cross stems.

Step 5. If volume is needed among the materials in the composition, use spreaders. Remember, no foliage below the binding point.

Step 6. Finish your bouquet with leaves, vines, or branches.

Step 7. Tie at the binding point with twine, raffia, or ribbon.

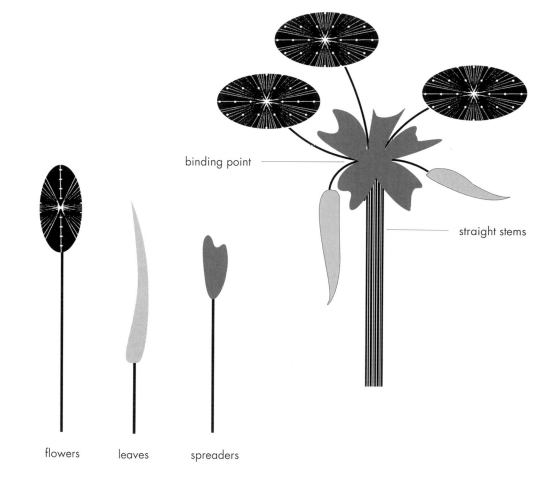

binding point

straight stems

flowers leaves spreaders

Straight-stem bouquet.

Completed contemporary
straight-stem bouquet in
tall glass vase.

Contemporary
straight-stem
bouquet, details.

WEAVING, WREATHS, AND ARMATURES

Nature is the original—not to mention the most skillful and playful—master of the weaver's art. Having by now understood that beauty comes when form follows function, it is easy to see why this is so. Weaving is a protective cover formed by the interlacing of materials; a wreath or armature is a skeletal frame by which a three-dimensional structure supports itself. Nature's versions of these forms rank among its most compelling creations. Vines twist themselves into ropes, which in turn enlace branches and trees, or secure themselves with clinging tendrils. Branches interlock with each other, and grasses make thick, protective mats on the surface of the ground. Ever functional, these are systems by which a plant can climb, spread, or brace and protect itself.

Wiring and binding techniques

Techniques of wiring and binding are integral to weaving and the construction of wreaths and armatures. If beautifully executed, these techniques can even be incorporated into the design concept for contemporary compositions. Good technique is essential from the very beginning of a construction; remember that these support systems will be visible unless you plan to cover them with moss or some other sort of camouflage. Neat,

Ulmus glabra 'Camperdownii' (Camperdown elm), Filoli Estate.

Manzanita armature.

simple joints and bindings can be easily concealed. Wrapping wire once around a joint or binding point has the advantage of being unobtrusive and clean—and makes just as strong a connection as multiple wraps.

A 28-gauge brass wire lends beautiful support that is also decorative. For a single tie, twist around once, finishing the ends by spiraling them around a pencil or piece of bamboo. For a cross tie, make a strong, elegant joint by binding crosswise in front and side to side in back. Gold thread makes a striking finish on the ends of visible supports, such as bamboo. Connections made with electrical ties are neat and strong and can be part of the composition in contemporary designs.

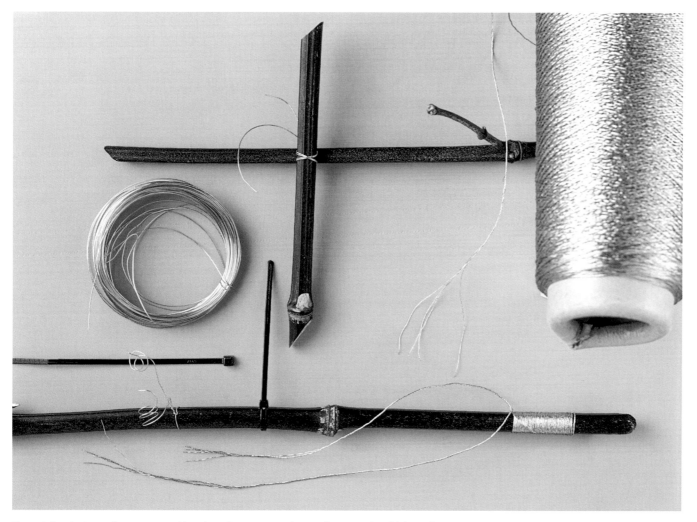

Essential techniques for wiring and binding: brass wire, electrical ties, and gold thread.

Living wreaths

Among the most striking and flexible wreaths are those whose support systems combine an armature with living plants. Ivy or other strong vines such as clematis, jasmine, honeysuckle, cestrum, trumpet, or passion flower look exceptionally beautiful when woven through armatures. Such living wreaths can last for weeks, giving the designer the option to add a variety of cut flowers, fruits, or berries to suit specific occasions over the course of time. The armature may be made of natural materials or, as is the case in the next design, a very practical wire wreath form.

To assemble this living wreath of a support system, wash the ivy thoroughly and weave one or more entire plants into the wire wreath form, inserting the roots first through the openings. Fill the container with water. Use this ivy wreath as a foundation for the stems of other plant material, combining full blooms, buds, berries,

Wire wreath forms and glass bowl.

or fruits to produce a rounded form that incorporates varied shapes (as in the Gallery, page 157). The entire structure can be lifted out of the container, allowing the water to be replaced easily.

For other armatures, see pages 164–165, 166–167, and 171 of the Gallery.

Weaving with grass

A simple woven collar placed around a votive candle holder can make a delightful informal container for individual bulbs or single flowers. Lily grass (*Liriope exiliflora*), one of the most beautiful and readily available grasses, is easy to work with and can last up to a week without water. Other materials, for example, flax (*Linum usitatissimum*), bullrushes (*Typha* spp.), or anything long, narrow, and flexible, can be used.

Ivy wreath on a glass bowl.

To assemble, first trim away the lower, rounded ends of the lily grass so that the blades can lie flat. Lay enough vertical lengths, tips all in one direction, to cover the circumference of candle holder. Then weave other lengths of grass over and under to make a flat mat. Turn the mat over and fold the cut ends back, using a low-heat glue gun to attach them to the nearest horizontal grass. Place the back side of the mat against the glass, and roll the mat around it. Glue the horizontal

Lily-grass weaving and the votive holder it will surround.

Paperwhite narcissus in a
collar of woven lily grass.

grasses on the side with the cut ends to the glass, and weave the tip ends of the other side back into the mat to hold the collar together. Spray with leaf gloss.

This technique can be modified to make a box-shaped basket (pages 220–221 of the Gallery). Other examples of weaving in the Gallery include calla lilies (pages 162–163) and a hanging weaving of wax flowers for a powder room (page 215).

The materials, techniques, and construction methods discussed in this chapter offer a broad instructional base for working with flowers. Once mastered, they can be used creatively on their own or become building blocks for more complicated compositions. These technical skills give you the confidence and knowledge with which to experiment. Combine them with others, or invent new ones. There is always room for improvement! The beauty of the flower will inspire you to find your own path in the art of floral design.

Photograph Gallery of Floral Design

There are many ways a flower guides us in the color, form, and function of a floral design. This Gallery displays a global variety in many roles, from the beauty of a single bloom to the pleasures of groupings, and in occasions both simple and grand. Using the concepts and techniques introduced in the previous chapters, it offers ideas for a broad spectrum of skill levels, styles, containers, and surroundings in designs ranging from almost botanical to nearly abstract. Lovely, versatile, and each one unique, it is easy to see why people have always chosen to celebrate life with flowers.

Vase of hand-hammered repoussé black
copper by Robert Kuo. Exclusively at
Gumps, San Francisco, California.

In a careful balance of complementary shapes, the rounded base, long neck, and subtle, nearly black coloration of this exquisite handmade vase highlight the slender stem, graceful leaves, ruffled petals, and brilliant coloration of a single hybrid tree peony

Materials: *Paeonia* 'Souvenir de Maxime Cornu'. Flower courtesy Filoli Estate; vase by Robert Kuo. Vase life: three days.

This grouping relies upon the principle of rhythm. The irregular organic shapes of the vases echo the irregular forms of the orchids. The containers' neutral colors and quietude make a natural pairing with the vibrant color and dancing movement of the flowers.

Materials: odontoglossums, handblown glass vases. Flowers courtesy Golden Gate Orchids, San Francisco, California; vases by Benjamin Edols and Kathy Elliot, courtesy De Vera, San Francisco, California. Vase life: two weeks.

Opposite A study of the color yellow and neutral white, graphic linearity is the theme of this composition. Even the outlines of the vases and orchid blooms play active roles.

Materials: cattleyas, paphiopedilums, phalaenopsis, phaius, handblown glass vases, tray. Flowers courtesy Golden Gate Orchids; vases and tray courtesy De Vera. Vase life: one week.

Overleaf In this deceptively simple composition, each flower must be placed so that it functions both as an individual actor and group participant whose color and rhythm interact with its companions.

Materials: tulips, driftwood (drilled and fitted with glass cylinders). Vase life: one week.

Flowers and container unite in a structural study of form, color, and line. The extravagantly ruffled blooms display a complex color scheme of both complementary and analogous harmonies.
In a contrast of extremes, the simplicity of the container and the fully visible, strongly stylized lines of the stems keep the blooms from looking overly busy.

Materials: assorted tall bearded iris, plexiglass container. Vase life: five days.

The informal playfulness characterizing the happiness of spring comes to life in this simple composition in which vases of different heights are unified through identical materials and color. No yellow is more cheerful than that of the narcissus.

Materials: narcissus, green glass vases. Vases by Heikki Orvolla, Iittala Glass Finland, courtesy Sam and Marianna Ferris. Vase life: four days.

As practical as it is pretty, this living wreath of ivy can be embellished with many types of cut flowers, lasts for weeks, and lends itself to a variety of occasions and settings. The wire frame permits water to be changed with ease.

Materials: hydrangeas, ivy, glass container, wire wreath form. Vase life: ivy, three weeks; hydrangeas, one week.

This selaginella moss planter is ideal for a quiet display and perfect as the centerpiece for an informal table setting. The flat geometry, neutral colors, and contrast of textures between the cheerful green moss and the metal container are restfully contemplative.

Materials: club moss (*Selaginella* spp.), aluminum platter, floral foam, liners. Vase life: two to four weeks.

An entirely different mood is achieved with the addition of lily of the valley pips or other small flowers. Here, clusters of fresh violets turn the simple composition into a festive celebration for a special occasion.

Materials: as opposite, with addition of violets (*Viola odorata*). Vase life of additional flowers: one day.

Opposite The graceful wrought iron stand offsets the weight and bulk of the thirty-six-inch-diameter antique Chinese container, whose shape and soft black coloration work well with the rounded green and white form of the azalea. This study in neutrals is strong enough to make a statement yet restful enough to be an island of calm.

Materials: 'Oregon Alaska' azalea, black clay container, wrought iron stand. Container and stand courtesy Living Green, San Francisco, California. Vase life: one month.

Overleaf A study in line and the color yellow, this design weaves materials through the screen, placing their stems in test tubes on the back. The unusual two-dimensional perspective emphasizes the linear quality of the composition.

Materials: calla lilies (*Zantedeschia* spp.), hala leaves (*Pandanus tectorius*), *Libertia grandiflora* berries, black bamboo (*Phyllostachys nigra*), woven willow screen, test tubes. Screen courtesy Willow Mania, Pescadero, California. Vase life: one week.

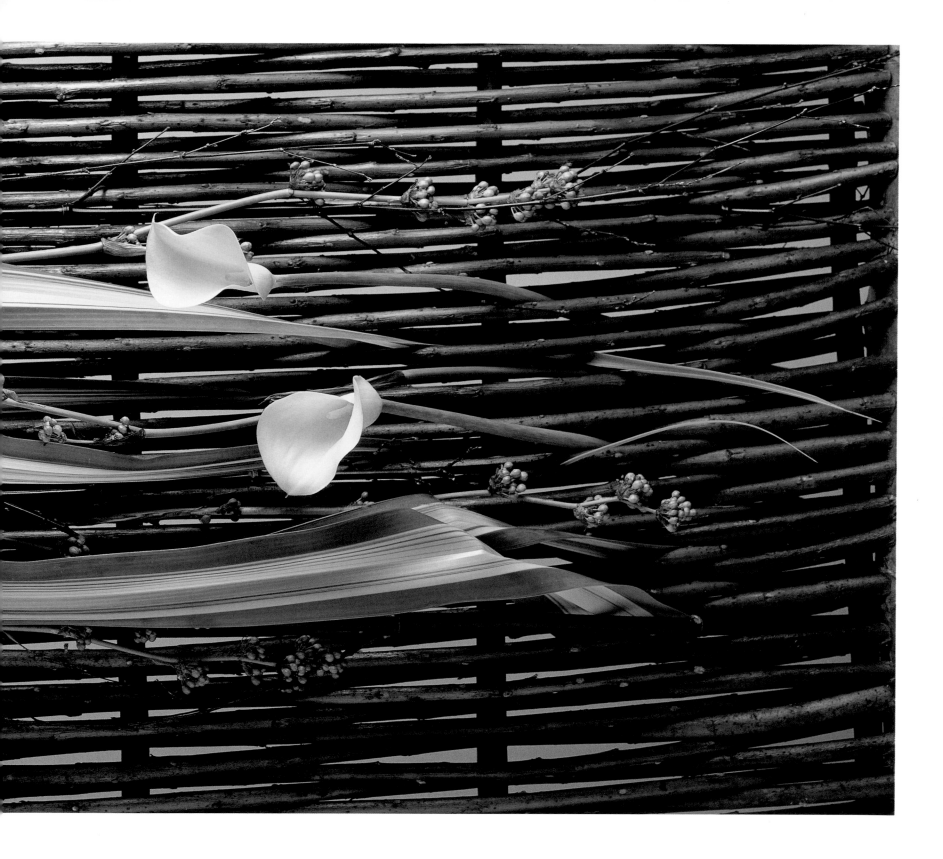

Opposite Carefully composed asymmetry and effective placement of counterbalanced forms between a whole orchid and the manzanita armature result in an unusual, eye-catching effect of weightlessness.

Materials: dendrobium, manzanita. Manzanita courtesy Columbia Pine Cones. Vase life: one month.

Overleaf In a symbiotic interplay of line, color, and shape, whole orchid plants grace a six-foot-long armature built from separate pieces of manzanita placed upside down. The small rounded shapes of the manzanita leaves echo the contours of the orchid flowers, while their green harmonizes with that of the flower stems. These in turn pick up the sinuous lines of the manzanita branches, whose warm brown blends with the yellow of the orchids.

Materials: *Oncidium* 'Gower Ramsey', manzanita (*Arctostaphylos* spp.). Manzanita courtesy Columbia Pine Cones, Columbia, California. Vase life: one month.

Opposite Dramatic elegance for a large contemporary space, this design requires advance planning. The downward arcs of the two orchid branches required weeks of training to achieve. Test tubes placed in the top of the seven-foot-tall vase hold blooms and eucalyptus, whose leaves pick up both the pattern of the vase and the playful lightness of the oncidium.

Materials: *Oncidium* Elegance 'Midas', eucalyptus, handmade ceramic vases, test tubes. Vases by Hedi K. Ernst, Oakland, California. Vase life: two weeks.

Left Trained oncidium, detail.

Opposite Floral design isn't always about flowers. Bare woven branches and vegetables can make beautifully expressive abstract compositions that maintain the integrity of the materials.

Materials: golden weeping willow (*Salix alba* 'Tristis'), yellow squash. Vase life: three months.

Overleaf Jewel-like arrangements in miniature glass vases celebrate the preciousness of newborn babies. The pretty containers become even more attractive when embellished with ribbon. Inexpensive and extremely versatile, they can be used in a variety of settings, either singly or in groups, such as for table decorations or even as a simple way for teaching children floral design.

Materials: small glass vases, ribbons, and (clockwise, from top left) dendrobiums; freesias; miniature floribunda spray roses; lily of the valley (*Convallaria majalis*); *Delphinium* Belladonna Group; monkshood (*Aconitum* spp.); forget-me-nots (*Myosotis scorpioides*); hydrangea; miniature floribunda spray roses; David Austin roses. Ribbons courtesy Shibata, San Francisco Flower Mart, San Francisco, California. Vase life: three to seven days.

Opposite The brilliant color and appealing texture of violets show how lively the versatile wreath can be.

Materials: violets (*Viola odorata*), wire wreath form, binding wire. Arrangement courtesy Año Nuevo Nursery, San Francisco Flower Mart. Vase life: one day.

Overleaf Dried fruits and flowers make arrangements that are as striking as they are long lasting. In the first wreath, the brilliant Chinese-red berries of hawthorn make a colorful study in geometric simplicity. In the second wreath, freeze-dried roses in shades of pink and peach and orange slices emphasize texture and analogous harmonies. In the third wreath, a della robbia, the mixed colors of a variety of dried fruits evoke autumn.

Materials: Styrofoam, wire wreath forms, and (from left) berries of hawthorn (*Crataegus* spp.); freeze-dried Ecuadorian roses and slices of navel orange (*Citrus sinensis*); pomegranates (*Punica granatum*), eucalyptus pods, rose hips, and slices of dried persimmon (*Diospyros kaki*) and navel orange (*Citrus sinensis*). Vase life: Wreath 1, two weeks; Wreaths 2 and 3, unlimited.

Opposite Open white roses make a wreath of lovely texture and subtle coloration appropriate for many sacred occasions.

Materials: *Rosa* 'Bianca', floral foam wreath form. Setting courtesy St. Peter's Chapel, Mare Island, California. Vase life: five days.

Overleaf Often, mothers of the bride have preferred small bouquets to corsages. Planned to harmonize with her dress, a mother's bouquet can make an exquisite yet bold, individualistic statement. A striking flower stands out with style on the father's lapel. These beautiful and assertive flowers highlight a parent's special place in the wedding party.

Materials: (left to right) yellow cattleyas; *Rosa* 'Sonora Sunset' (boutonniere); *Rosa* 'Sonora Sunset', *R.* 'Toscanini', and *R.* 'Fragrant Fantasy'; fuchsia cattleyas. Vase life: one day.

Above and opposite The lily of the valley's unique expression of texture, fragrance, and color say "purity and simplicity." Combined with antique silk ribbon, it speaks of the ideal wedding bouquet.

Materials: lily of the valley (*Convallaria majalis*). Ribbon courtesy Britex, San Francisco, California. Vase life: once completed, good for wedding day.

Overleaf Four variations on hand-tied technique show its versatility. Each of these four bridesmaids' bouquets is designed in keeping with the style of the wedding, to harmonize with the bridesmaids' dresses, and to highlight the bride.

Materials: (left to right) black calla lilies (*Arum palaestinum*); hydrangeas and viburnum berries; Ecuadorian roses; David Austin roses. Ribbons courtesy Britex, San Francisco. Vase life: one day.

A white theme, appropriate for a wedding, highlights the exquisite Tiffany stained-glass windows and the serene Arts and Crafts–style beauty of St. Peter's Chapel.

Materials: hydrangeas, *Rosa* 'Bianca', Japanese anemone (*Anemone* ×*hybrida*), glaucous maidenhair fern (*Adiantum latifolium*), terra cotta containers, extenders. Setting courtesy St. Peter's Chapel; candles courtesy Creative Candles, Kansas City, Missouri.

The fourteen-foot height of this arrangement, which incorporates the baptismal font, brings the beautiful ceiling of the sanctuary actively into the composition and draws the eye to the magnificent circular window.

Materials: Japanese anemones (*Anemone ×hybrida*), glaucous maidenhair fern (*Adiantum latifolium*), terra cotta containers, extenders. Setting courtesy St. Peter's Chapel; candles courtesy Creative Candles. Vase life: one week.

Lustrous whites and greens make a neutral yet dramatic foil for the luminous hues of the chapel's rear window, where twelve towering feet of graceful blooms catch the eye, welcoming wedding party and guests.

Materials: Japanese anemones (*Anemone ×hybrida*), glaucous maidenhair fern (*Adiantum latifolium*), extenders, terra cotta container. Setting courtesy St. Peter's Chapel; candles courtesy Creative Candles. Vase life: one week.

The floral theme is repeated in low planters along the pews to integrate visually the entire sanctuary in the scheme of elegant neutral colors and lacy textures without distracting the eye from the glorious stained-glass windows.

Materials: hydrangea plants, glaucous maidenhair fern (*Adiantum latifolium*) plants, terra cotta containers. Setting courtesy St. Peter's Chapel. Vase life: one month.

Opposite Madrone, oregano, and small roses delicately accent the spun-sugar veil and are repeated in the miniature bouquet of a marzipan bride and her groom's boutonniere. They grace a wedding cake above a table carpeted with fragrant gardenias.

Materials: floribunda spray roses, madrone (*Arbutus menziesii*), oregano (*Origanum vulgare*), cape jessamine (*Gardenia augusta*). Cake courtesy Masse's Pastries, Berkeley, California. Vase life: one day.

Overleaf Having a different color combination at each table added to the lively and joyous atmosphere of the reception. Such variety is very effective in the open conditions and natural light of a late afternoon supper outdoors.

Materials: *Phlox paniculata*, dahlias, scabiosa, trachelium, floribunda spray roses, Ecuadorian roses, hydroponic roses, borage (*Borago officinalis*), oregano (*Origanum vulgare*), glass cylinders. Vase life: four to five days.

This bride adored all colors, so we obliged, as did the chef, who used some of the edible flowers in the salad.

Setting courtesy Crocker Mansion, Hillsborough, California.

No flower expresses tradition and beauty better than a rose. Here, three dishes on a branching pedestal make a graceful container for a magnificent arrangement of hybrid blooms, including David Austin roses. Highlighted by mango-colored candles, their tints, ranging from yellow through brandy to pale and deep pink, harmonize with the soft hue of the walls. Richness of texture, color, and fragrance complement a setting in which the contrast of antiques in deep lustrous woods and silver create an ambience of sophisticated elegance.

Materials: David Austin roses, garden roses, heirloom silver. Setting courtesy Margaret Lee Blunt; flowers courtesy The Gardens at Heather Farm, Walnut Creek, California; candles courtesy Creative Candles, Kansas City, Missouri. Vase life: four days.

Focal points of relatively low height, these center-pieces harmonize with the white-dominated pattern of the Japanese obi; the dark eyes of the anemones pick up the black accents of the brocade. The designs do not compete with the surroundings or impede dinner conversation, but along with the candles provide understated elegance.

Materials: freesias, bleeding heart (*Dicentra spec-tabilis*), hydrangeas, tulips, anemones, snowball viburnum, brunia foliage. Setting courtesy Filoli Estate; candles courtesy Creative Candles, Kansas City, Missouri. Vase life: five days.

Brilliant color and opulent texture make a bold statement suitable for an austerely elegant dining room setting dominated by neutrals and glass. The nearly flat pool of pure hue harmonizes with the painting and gains extra impact from its reflection in the glass tabletop. An ideal height, this centerpiece will not interfere with dinner conversation.

Materials: hybrid tuberous begonias, plexiglass container. Setting courtesy Alfred and Hedi Schmid-Ernst. Vase life: two days.

Conceived as a total setting, the potted plant garden and loose open bouquet combined with the rustic informality of willow furniture call for a relaxing afternoon. White and blue wonderfully complement the water off this houseboat and give this setting a refreshing feel.

Materials: queen anne's lace (*Ammi majus*), marguerite daisies (*Argyranthemum frutescens*), matilija poppies (*Romneya coulteri*), the blue berries of *Dianella tasmanica*, grasses, agapanthus, iris, glass vase, terra cotta pots. Setting courtesy Richard and Luisiana Galle; willow furniture courtesy Willow Mania, Pescadero, California; styling by Milena Boucher, San Francisco, California. Vase life: one week.

Breakfast in bed celebrates Sunday morning.
Mature Ecuadorian roses pick up the color of the
linens and accent the fruit cups.

Materials: *Rosa* 'Yellow Submarine', glass basket.
Setting courtesy Richard and Luisiana Galle; styling
by Milena Boucher, San Francisco, California.
Vase life: one week.

Opulent and graceful, this traditional composition harmonizes with its surroundings. The pedestal brings its height into scale with the ballroom. Nuances of pinks and peaches pick up the sunrise colors of the murals, the yellows highlight the gold trim, and the foliage blends with the green walls. These soft hues come alive for nighttime festivities.

Materials: cherry blossoms (*Prunus* spp.), rhododendrons, lilacs (*Syringa* spp.), French tulips, floribunda spray roses, aucuba foliage, antique brass container. Setting courtesy Filoli Estate. Vase life: one week.

In the striking suspended container, the bright color of the rose hips and the delicate linearity of Chilean jasmine seedpods make a unifying transition to the abstract painting and playful chair, creating a compositional study based upon repetition of shape and line.

Materials: rose hips, seedpods of Chilean jasmine (*Mandevilla laxa*), handmade glass vase sculpture. Setting courtesy Alfred and Hedi Schmid-Ernst; vase courtesy Boris Jeanrenaud. Vase life: three to four weeks.

The classic shape and sparkling clarity of glass test tubes accent the graceful beauty of this hanging stephanotis weaving. A neutral coloration assures that the design will not be too busy. Even a small windowless space like this guest powder room can be made arrestingly attractive with the right floral display.

Materials: wax flowers (*Stephanotis floribunda*), test tubes, black string. Setting courtesy Alfred and Hedi Schmid-Ernst. Vase life: three to four days.

In general, a design should enhance its setting by harmonizing with it. Here, the rich coloration of the interior and outdoors suggested the hues of the composition, which gains distinction by its focus on the bright green color and simple striking shapes of the gourds. Well-composed groupings result from a formal theme, in this case the inter play of the rounded shapes of the berries, gourds, containers, and fruit. An appealing contrast is displayed in the sophisticated color, slender verticality, and bright points of light from the elegant candles.

Materials: glory lilies (*Gloriosa superba* 'Roths-childiana'), berries of madrone (*Arbutus menziesii*), persimmons (*Diospyros kaki*), gourds (drilled and fitted with test tubes and steadied by self-adhesive acrylic pads). Setting and vases courtesy Douglas and Mary Horngrad; candles courtesy Creative Candles, Kansas City, Missouri. Vase life: one week.

Above and opposite A season can be brought to mind even with an unusual choice of bloom. This unconventional bouquet mingles lilies, hydrangeas, and roses—usually associated with summer—with fall fruits and foliage. Enriched by the deep tones of the bronze container, they create an autumnal theme.

Materials: *Lilium* 'Barbaresco', *L.* 'Broadway', *L.* 'Girosa', *Rosa* 'Judy', persimmons (*Diospyros kaki*), bittersweet (*Solanum dulcamara*), cestrum, hydrangeas, viburnum foliage, bronze container. Container courtesy Archie Held, Richmond, California. Vase life: five days.

Overleaf This grouping of pomegranates and woven boxes is a metaphor for what I hope this book has become: a container of inspiration, fruitful with the seeds of creative ideas for every reader.

Materials: lily grass (*Liriope exiliflora*), pomegranates (*Punica granatum*), Styrofoam cubes, components for weaving techniques. Vase life: two weeks.

Suggested Reading

Art

Barrow, John D. 1995. *The Artful Universe.* Boston: Little, Brown & Co.

Hickman, Money, and Yasuhiro Satō. 1989. *The Paintings of Jakuchū.* New York: Harry N. Abrams.

Itten, Johannes. 1997. *The Art of Color: The Subjective Experience and Objective Rationale of Color.* Translated by Ernst von Haagen. New York: John Wiley and Sons.

Kemp, Martin. 1990. *The Science of Art.* New Haven, Conn.: Yale University Press.

Segal, Sam. 1990. *Flowers and Nature: Netherlandish Flower Paintings of Four Centuries.* Amstelveen, Netherlands: Hijnk International, b.v.

Shlain, Leonard. 1990. *Art and Physics: Parallel Visions in Space, Time and Light.* New York: William Morrow and Co.

Winkelmann-Rhein, Gertraude. 1969. *The Paintings and Drawings of Jan "Flower" Bruegel.* New York: Harry N. Abrams.

Color

Color. 1980. London: Marshall Editions, Ltd.

Gilliat, Mary. 1985. *The Mary Gilliat Book of Color.* Toronto: Octopus Books, Ltd., Little, Brown & Co.

Kaufman, Donald, and Taffy Dahl. 1992. *Color: Natural Palettes for Painted Rooms.* New York: Clarkson Potter Publishers.

———. 1998. *Color and Light.* New York: Crown Publishing.

McDonald, Elvin. 1995. *The Color Garden: White, Red, Yellow, Blue.* San Francisco: Collins Publishers.

Floral design

American Institute of Floral Designers. 1999. *Book of Floral Terminology*. Baltimore: American Institute of Floral Designers.

Guild, Tricia. 1998. *Guild Cut Flowers*. New York: Clarkson Potter Publishing.

———. 1996. *Tricia Guild in Town*. New York: Rizzoli International.

Huang, Yung-Chuan. 1988. *The Art of Traditional Chinese Flower Arranging*. Translated by Carolyn J. Phillips. San Francisco: The Asian Art Museum of San Francisco and the National Museum of History, Taipei, R.O.C.

Maia, Ronaldo. 1991. *More Decorating with Flowers*. New York: Harry N. Abrams.

Pritchard, Tom, and Billy Jarecki. 1985. *Flowers Rediscovered*. New York: Stewart, Tabori & Chang.

Sato, Shozo. 1966. *The Art of Arranging Flowers: A Complete Guide to Japanese Ikebana*. New York: Harry N. Abrams.

Van Doesburg, Jan. 1989. *Decorative & Vegetative Bloemsierkunst*. Zutphen, Netherlands: Terra.

Wegener, Ursula, and Paul Wegener. 1981. *Blumenkunst: Geschichte, Lehren, Proxis*. Munich: BLV Verlagsgesellschaft.

Nature studies

Doczi, György. 1981. *The Power of Limits: Proportional Harmonies in Nature, Art and Architecture*. Boulder, Colo.: Shambhala.

Malitz, Jerome, and Seth Malitz. 1998. *Reflecting Nature: Garden Designs from Wild Landscapes*. Portland, Ore.: Timber Press.

McNulty, Tim. 1998. *The Art of Nature: Reflections on the Grand Design*. New York: Barnes & Noble.

Nuridsany, Claude, and Marie Pèrennou. 1998. *The Metamorphosis of Flowers*. New York: Harry N. Abrams.

Plant and flower identification and care

Bechtel, Helmut. 1992. *The Manual of Cultivated Orchid Species*. 3d ed. Cambridge, Mass.: M.I.T. Press.

Griffiths, Mark. 1994. *The New Royal Horticultural Society Index of Garden Plants*. Portland, Ore.: Timber Press.

Ikebana International. 1997. *Tips for Longer Life of Ikebana Materials*. San Francisco: San Francisco Bay Area Chapter 31, Ikebana International.

Love, Gilly. 1994. *The Illustrated Encyclopedia of Cut Flowers*. London: Headline Book Publishing, Ltd.

Pridgeon, Alec, ed. 1992. *The Illustrated Encyclopedia of Orchids*. Portland, Ore.: Timber Press.

Society of American Florists. 1997. *Flower and Plant Care Manual*. Alexandria, Va.: Society of American Florists.

Index

Illustrations or photographs are indicated by **boldfaced** page numbers.

abstract design. See design

abstraction, 64

accent, 45, **47**

Aconitum (monkshood), 170, **172–173**

acrylic pads (Bump-ONs), 83, **83**, **89**, 216, **217**

Adiantum latifolium (glaucous maidenhair fern), 186, **187**, 188, **189**, 190, **191**, 192, **193**

agapanthus, 206, **207**

Agave, 32, 34
  franzosinii, **36**
  victoriae-reginae, and pattern, 30, **31**

allium, **76**, 77

alternative construction, 93, **93**

amaryllis. See *Hippeastrum*

American Institute of Floral Designers (A.I.F.D.), 44

Ammi majus (queen anne's lace), 206, **207**

analogous harmony. See color

Anemone ×*hybrida* (Japanese anemone), 186, **187**, 188, **189**, 190, **191**, 202, **203**

angel's trumpet datura. See *Brugmansia arborea*

angiosperm, 48

anther, 38, **49**

appreciation. See color, with form and appreciation

Arbutus menziesii (madrone), 194, **195**, 216, **216–217**

Archimedes spiral. See spiral

Arctostaphylos (manzanita), 104, **134**, 164, **164–167**

Argyranthemum frutescens (marguerite daisy), 206, **207**

armature, 104, **105**, 106, 134, 136, 137, 164, **164–167**

arm bouquet. See bouquet, bridesmaid's

Arum palaestinum (black calla lily), 182, **184–185**

asymmetry, 45, 62, 164, **164–165**

aucuba. See foliage

azalea, 'Oregon Alaska', 160, **161**

balance, 16, 18, 20, 30, 32
  with proportion, scale, and depth, 44, 45, **47**

bamboo. See *Phyllostachys*

bamboo, heavenly. See *Nandina domestica*

begonia, tuberous, 204, **205**

binding point, 108, 109, 116

binomial, 55

bittersweet. See *Solanum dulcamara*

black bamboo. See *Phyllostachys nigra*

black calla lily. See *Arum palaestinum*

blade, leaf, 48, 62

bleeding heart. See *Dicentra spectabilis*

blending, 20, 70

borage. See *Borago officinalis*

Borago officinalis (borage), 194, **195–197**

botanical design. See design

bouquet, 218, **218–219**
  bridesmaid's, **116–130**, 182, **184–185**
  hand-tied, 108, 109–111
  mother of the bride, 178, **180–181**
  presentation, **110–115**
  vase, 170, **172–173**
  wedding, 116, 182, **182–183**

boutonniere, 178, **180–181**

bracken fern. See *Pteridium aquilinum*

brass wire. See wire

bridal bouquet. See bouquet

Brueghel, Jan, 60–62; *Little Bouquet in a Clay Jar*, **56**

Brugmansia arborea (angel's trumpet datura), 20, **21**
brunia, 202, **203**
bulbs, 97–98, **99**, 100, 102, **103**, 137
bullrush. See *Typha*

cactus. See *Cereus*
cage
　funeral, **90**
　igloo, **90**
calla lily. See *Zantedeschia*
　black. See *Arum palaestinum*
calyx, 48, **49**, 106, 109
Camperdown elm. See *Ulmus glabra*
　'Camperdownii'
cape jessamine. See *Gardenia augusta*
cattleya, 148, **149**, **178**
centerpieces, 100, **101, 158**, 194, **196–197**, 199, 202, **203**, 204, **205**
Cereus (cactus), 26, **27**
cestrum, 218, **218–219**
cherry blossom. See *Prunus*
chicken wire. See wire
Chilean jasmine. See *Mandevilla laxa*
Chinese design. See design
chrysanthemum, 48
Citrus sinensis (navel orange), 174, **176–177**
clematis. See wreaths, living
climate, 38
club moss. See moss, selaginella
coil spiral. See spiral
color, 16, 34, 40, 42, 45, 46, **47**, 59, 60, 64, 65, 70, 73, **74**, 79, 97
　analogous harmony, 67, 73, 152, **153**
　combinations, 16
　complementary, 18, 20, 38, 66, **66**, 67
　composition, 16
　contrast, 67, 70, 73
　cool, 18, 67
　with form and appreciation, 57, 58
　with form and function, **15**, 44, 55, 64

harmony, 16, 20, 67, 70
hue, 66, **66**, 83
and light, 18–22, 38
monochromatic harmony, 67, 70, 73, 152, 153
neutral, 20, 22, 65
primary, 66
secondary, 66, 67
shades, 66, **66**
tertiary, 66, 67
and texture, 40
tints, 66, **66**, 73
tones, 66, **66**
warm, 18, 67, 70
Color Rendering Index (C.R.I.), 78
color shift, 75
color temperature, 75, 78
color wheel, 66, **66**, 67
composition, 32, 44, 45, **47**, 61
conditioning, 87, 88, 116
construction, materials and techniques, **89–90**, 91–98, **91–95**
container, 44, 45, 60, 61, 78–84, **80–81**, 91, 92, 97, 102, **103**, 109, 137, 200, 210, **211**, 212, **213**
　alternative, **94–95, 150**
　aluminum, **158–159**
　bronze, 218, **218–219**
　glass, 79, **103, 148**, 194, **195–197, 207**, 214, **215**
　gourds, **83**, 216, **216–217**
　planters, 160, **161**, 190, **191**
　Plexiglas, 152, **153**, 204, **205**
　test tubes, 160, **161, 168, 214–216**
contemporary design. See design
contrast, opposition, and tension, 45, **47**, 62, 70
Convallaria majalis (lily of the valley), 42, **43**, 108, 159, 170, **172–173**, 182, **182–183**
Cornus (dogwood), 93, 98, 104

corolla, 48, **49**
corsage, 109
corsage stem, 109
Crataegus (hawthorn), 174, **176–177**
cultivar, 55
curly willow, **88**, 93, **93**, 94, **94**, 98, 104

dahlia, 194, **195–197**
daisy
　gerbera, 66, 67, **68–69**, 70, 73, **76**, 77, 78
　marguerite. See *Argyranthemum frutescens*
dandelion, 32
datura, angel's trumpet. See *Brugmansia arborea*
della robbia, 174, **176**
Delphinium, **76**, 77, 170, **172–173**
dendrobium, 104, 164, **164–165**, 170, **172–173**
depth, 20, 24, 28, 45, **47**
design
　abstract, 64, 65, 170
　botanical, 61, 64
　Chinese, 58, 59
　contemporary, 64
　elements of, 16–17, 18, 44
　European, 59, 60
　Japanese, 58, 59
　principles of, 16–17, 18, 44
designer block, **91**
Dianella tasmanica, 206, 207
Dicentra spectabilis (bleeding heart), 202, **203**
dicotyledon, 48
dimension, 45
Diospyros kaki (persimmon), 174, **176–177**, 216, 218, **216–219**
dogwood. See *Cornus*
dominance, emphasis, accent, and focal point, 45, **47**
dusty miller, 73

Ecuadorian rose. See *Rosa*

electrical ties, 93

elements and principles of design, 16–17, 44

elm, Camperdown. See *Ulmus glabra* 'Camperdownii'

emphasis, 45, **47**, 60

equiangular spiral. See spiral

eucalyptus, 32, 73, 168, **168–169**, 174, **176–177**

European design. See design

extender, 92, 186, **187**, 188, **189**

fern
  bracken. See *Pteridium aquilinum*
  glaucous maidenhair. See *Adiantum latifolium*

Fibonacci Series, 30, **32**, 34

filament, 44

filler, 110, 116, **117**

finisher, 110, 116, **117**

floral care, 87–91

floral foam, **89–90**, 91–92, 94, 95, **158–159**, 178

floral tape, **89**, 91, 106, 109

flower, structure of, 16, 26, 48, **49**

focal point, 45, 46, **47**, 58, 75, 78, 202, **203**

foliage, 18, 42, 100, 102
  aucuba, 210, **211**
  brunia, 202, **203**
  viburnum, 218, **218–219**

forget-me-not. See *Myosotis scorpioides*

form, 15, 16, 22–24, 44, 46, 55, 57, 58, 59, 60, 62, 64, 97, 146

fragrance, 42, 44, 65

Freesia, 170, **172–173**, 202, **203**
  alba, **103**

fritillaria, 61

function, 48

funeral cage, **91**

funeral cone, 88, **89**

funnel, 92

galax, 111, **111**

Gardenia augusta (cape jessamine), 194, **195**

genus, 55

gerbera, 66, 67, **68–69**, 70, 73, **76**, 77, 78

ginger, ornamental. See *Zingiber*

Gloriosa superba 'Rothschildiana' (glory lily), 216, **216–217**

glory lily. See *Gloriosa superba* 'Rothschildiana'

Goethe, Johann Wolfgang von, 15, 18

Golden Mean, 30

Golden Ratio, 30, **32**

Golden Rectangle, 30

Golden Section, 30

Golden Spiral, 30

golden weeping willow. See *Salix alba* 'Tristis'

gold thread, 98, 135, **135**

gourds, 83, **83**, 170, **171**, 216, **216–217**

grande block, **91**

grape hyacinth. See *Muscari latifolium*

grass, 48, 206, **207**
  lily. See *Liriope exiliflora*

green, as a neutral, 18, 20, 34, 66, 67

grid, 93, **93**

hala. See *Pandanus tectorius*

hand-tie, 109–111, 116–117
  spiral, 111, **112**, 116
  straight-stem, 131, **131–133**

hardening, 87

harmony, 15, 16, 18, 44, 46, **47**, 58, 79, 216, **216–217**

hawthorn. See *Crataegus*

heavenly bamboo. See *Nandina domestica*

Hedera (ivy), 136, **137**, 156, **157**

Heliconia vellerigera, **132–133**

Hippeastrum (amaryllis), 98, **99**

honeysuckle vine. See wreaths, living

hue. See color

hyacinth, 61, 97

hybrid, 55

hydrangea, 62, **110**, 111, 117, 156, **157**, 170, **172–173**, 182, **184–185**, 186, **187**, 192, **193**, 202, **203**, 218, **218–219**

igloo cage, **91**

ikebana, 58

inflorescence, **49**, 61, 111

iris, 32
  bearded, 60, 61, 97, **153**, 206, **207**

Itten, Johannes, 44

Itō Jakuchū, 60, 61; *Rooster, Hen and Hydrangeas*, 62, **63**, 64, 65

Itō Jakuen, 65; *Banana Leaves*, 65, **65**

ivy. See *Hedera*

Japanese anemone. See *Anemone ×hybrida*

Japanese design. See design

jasmine. See wreaths, living

Kelvin scale, 75, 78

lady slipper orchid. See orchid

leaf, 48, **50–54**, 65, 67
  compound, 48, **51**
  simple, 48, **51**

leaf margins, 53

leaf shapes, **50**, **52**

leaf surfaces, **54**

leaf venations, **50**

leaves, 28, 32, 34, 38, 48, 52, 73, 102, 109, 111, **111**, **218–219**

Leucospermum (pincushion protea), 40, **41**

Libertia grandiflora, 160, **162–163**

lichen
  Sierra, 88, **89**
  Spanish, 88, **89**

light, 16, 20, 22, 34 45, 58, 65, 75–78, **76**
   artificial, **76**, 77, 78
   candle-, **76**
   day-, 75, **76**, 77, 78
   fluorescent, **76**, 77, 78
   incandescent, 75, **76**, 77, 78
lilacs. See *Syringa*
Lilium (lily), 48, 61, 111
   'Barbaresco', 218, **218–219**
   'Broadway', 218, **218–219**
   'Girosa', 218, **218–219**
   stargazer, 111, **111**
lily. See *Lilium*
lily grass. See *Liriope exiliflora*
lily of the valley. See *Convallaria majalis*
line, 26–30, 46, **47**
liner, 90, 94, 95, **158**
Linnaean binomial system, 55
Liriope exiliflora (lily grass), 102, **103**, 137, **138–139**, 218, **220–221**
London plane tree. See *Platanus ×hispanica*
lupine, 32

madrona. See *Arbutus menziesii*
Magnolia, 65
   'Elizabeth', 15
   ×*soulangeana*, 15, 22, **23**, 24, **25**, 46, **47**, 48
maidenhair fern, glaucous. See *Adiantum latifolium*
Mandevilla laxa (Chilean jasmine), 212, **213**
manzanita. See *Arctostaphylos*
marguerite daisy. See *Argyranthemum frutescens*
marigold, 61
materials for floral design, **89**, **90**
matilija poppy. See *Romneya coulteri*
mechanics, 129
monkshood. See *Aconitum*
monochromatic harmony. See color
monocotyledon, 48

moss, 88, **89**, 91, 134
   Iceland, 88, **89**
   mood, 88, **89**
   selaginella, 95, **95**, **158–159**
   sheet, 88, **89**, 104
   Spanish, 88, **89**
   sphagnum, 88, **89**, 104
moth orchid. See orchid
multiple-flower stem. See stem
Muscari latifolium (grape hyacinth), 61, **86**
Myosotis scorpioides (forget-me-not), 170, **172–173**

Nandina domestica (heavenly bamboo), **132**
Narcissus, 26, 60, 61, 97, 154, **155**
   papyraceus (paperwhite narcissus), **97**, **139**
navel orange. See *Citrus sinensis*
neutrals, 20, 62, 65, 98, 79, 102, **103**, 146, **148**, **158**, 160, **161**, 190, **191**, 192, **193**, 204, **205**, 214, **215**

odontoglossum, **146–147**
oncidium, 104
   Elegance 'Midas', 168, **168–169**
   'Gower Ramsey', **166–167**
opposition, 45, **47**
orchid
   cattleya, 148, **149**, **178**
   dendrobium, 104, 164, **164–165**, 170, **172–173**
   odontoglossum, **146–147**
   oncidium, 104, **166–167**, 168, **168–169**
   paphiopedilum (lady slipper orchid), 148, **149**
   phaius, 148, **149**
   phalaenopsis (moth orchid), 104, **105**, 148, **149**
oregano. See *Origanum vulgare*
Origanum vulgare (oregano), 194, **195–197**
ovary, 48, **49**

Paeonia 'Souvenir de Maxime Cornu' (tree peony), **144**
Pandanus tectorius (hala), 160, **162–163**
paperwhite narcissus. See *Narcissus papyraceus*
paphiopedilum (lady slipper orchid), 148, **149**
papier-mâché, **91**
passion flower vine. See wreaths, living
pattern, 28–34, 46, 73
   explosion (sphere), 32, **33**
   fractal, 32, **33**
peony. See *Paeonia*
perianth, 48, **49**
persimmon. See *Diospyros kaki*
perspective, 45
petal, 15, 20, 34, 38, 48, **49**, 61, 67, 70
petiole, 48
phaius, 148, **149**
phalaenopsis (moth orchid), 104, **105**, 148, **149**
philodendron, **132**
Phlox paniculata, 194, **195–197**
Phyllostachys (bamboo)
   green, 88, 92, **92**, 100, 104, 135
   nigra (black), 97, 98, 160, **162–163**
pincushion flower. See *Scabiosa caucasica*
pincushion protea. See *Leucospermum*
pistil, 15, 38, 48, **49**
pittosporum, **110–111**, 111
pivot point. See binding point
plane tree, London. See *Platanus ×hispanica*
Platanus ×hispanica (London plane tree, sycamore), 18, **19**
pomegranate. See *Punica granatum*
poppy, matilija. See *Romneya coulteri*
presentation bouquet. See bouquet
proportion, 28, 45, **47**
protea, pincushion. See *Leucospermum*
Prunus (cherry), 210, **211**

Pteridium aquilinum, 32
Punica granatum (pomegranate), 174, **176–177**, 218, **220–221**

queen anne's lace. See *Ammi majus*

"reading nature," 16, 18, 24, 46, 55, 60, 64, 65, 67
repetition, 30, 46, **47**
rhododendron, 210, **211**
Rhus (sumac), **110–111**, 111
rhythm, 16, 30
  with transition, repetition, and variation, 45, 46, **47**, 146, **150–151**
ribbon, 70, 73, 170, **172–173**, 182, **182–185**
Romneya coulteri (matilija poppy), 206, 207
Rosa (rose), 26, 44, 48, 61, 70, 73, 106, 109, 111, 178, **179**
  'Bianca', 178, **179**, 186, **187**
  David Austin, 170, **172–173**, 182, **184–185**, 200, **200–201**
  Ecuadorian, 111, **111**, **117**, **176–177**, 182, **184–185**, 194, **195–197**
  floribunda spray, 111, **111**, 117, 170, **172–173**, 194, **195–197**, 210, **211**
  'Fragrant Fantasy', 178, **180–181**
  garden, 200, **200–201**
  hydroponic, 194, **195–197**
  'Judy', 218, **218–219**
  'Sonora Sunset', 178, **180–181**
  'Toscanini', 178, **180–181**
  'Yellow Submarine', 208, **209**
rose hip, 28, **29**, 170, **176–177**, 212, **213**

Salix (willow)
  alba 'Tristis' (golden weeping willow), 104, 170, **171**
  curly, **88**, 93, **93**, 94, **94**, 98, 104
  screen, 160, **162–163**

Scabiosa caucasica (pincushion flower), 34, 38, 194, **196–197**
scale, 45, **47**
season, 34–42
selaginella. See moss
sepal, 15, 28, 34, 48, **49**, 61
shade. See color
shape, 24–26, **47**, 60, 61, 62, 64, 65, 97
single-flower stem. See stem
size, 28–34, 45, 46, **47**, 61
snowball viburnum. See viburnum
Society of American Florists, 91
Solanum dulcamara (bittersweet), 218, **218–219**
space, 24, 26–30, 46, 65
species, 55
specific epithet, 55
spectrum, 67, 75
sphagnum moss. See moss
spiral
  Archimedes, 32, **33**
  coil, 32, **33**
  equiangular, **33**
spiral hand tie. See hand-tie
split complement, 66, **66**
spreader, 110, **110**, **111**, 116, 117
stamen, 15, 48, **49**, 61
stargazer lily, 111, **111**
stem, 28, 48, 61, 67, 79, 88, 98, 100, 103, 106, 108, 109
  multiple-flower, **49**, 110, 116
  single-flower, 110, 117
Stephanotis floribunda (wax flower), 214, **215**
stigma, 48, **49**
stitch leaf wiring, 109
straight-stem hand-tie. See hand-tie
structure, 15, 26, 30, 48, 55
style, 48, **49**
Styrofoam, 174, **176–177**, 218, **220–221**

sumac. See *Rhus*
support, 98
sycamore. See *Platanus ×hispanica*
symmetry, 45
Syringa (lilac), 210, **211**

taping. See wiring and taping techniques
tension, 45, **47**
textiles, 70, 73, **74**
texture, 16, 20, 34, 40, 45, 46, **47**, 61, 73, 79, 83, 97, 100, **158**, 174, 178, 192, **193**, 204, **205**
tint. See color
tokonoma, 58
tone. See color
trachelium, 194, **195–197**
transition, 46, **47**, 60, 65, 117
tree peony, **144**
triad, 66, **66**
  of color, form, and function, 44, 55
trumpet vine. See wreaths, living
tying. See hand-tie
Typha (bullrush), 137
Tulipa (tulip), 38, 61, 97, 106, **150–151**, 202, 203
  French, 210, **211**
  'Hella Light', **96**

Ulmus glabra 'Camperdownii' (Camperdown elm), **134**
unity, 16, 44, **47**, 55

variation, 46, **47**
vase bouquet. See bouquet
viburnum, 182, **184–185**
  snowball, 202, **203**
Viola odorata (violet), 48, **76**, 77, 97, **159**, 174, **175**
violet. See *Viola odorata*

water source, 87, 88, 91, 116

wax flower. See *Stephanotis floribunda*

weaving, 67, 134, **134**, 137–140, **138**, 170, **171**, 214, **215**, 218, **220–221**

weddings, 73, 92, 93, 106, 109, 116–130, **116–130**, 131, **131, 179–199**

willow. See *Salix*

wire
   binding, 174, **175**

brass, 98, 135, **135**

chicken, **90**, 92, 93, **93**

enameled, 106, **107–108**

wreath forms, 136, **137**, 156, **157**, 174, **175–177**

wiring and taping techniques, 106–109, **107**, 134–135, **135**

wisteria, 47

wreaths, 70, **71, 72**, 73, 88–94, 134
   living, **136**, 156, **157**, 174, **175–177**, 178, **179**

Zantedeschia (calla lily), 160, **162–163**

Zingiber (ornamental ginger), 38, **40**